IN HIS OWN WORDS

"Never once in my life have I referred to myself as H. Ross Perot. My friends don't call me H. Ross. Even my enemies don't call me that."

❑

"Japan is our rival, not our enemy. Japan is a competitor. Bashing a Toyota won't make a better car."

❑

"I am sort of like the fellow standing by the side of the road. A Cadillac pulled up and the driver asked him if he knew where New Boston was. The fellow answered no. The driver asked if he knew where Gladewater was, and he said he didn't know. This fellow in the Cadillac said, 'What in the world do you know?' The old fellow answered, 'I know I am not lost.'"

❑

"Isn't it bizarre that the only heroes from [Dese[illegible] [illegible]iticians?"

"We'[illegible] has stopped beati[illegible] toes, and all the politicians want to talk about is the fingers and toes. I want to go straight to the heart."

ROSS PEROT

In His Own Words

BY TONY CHIU

A Time Warner Company

If you purchase this book without a cover you should be aware that this book may have been stolen property and reported as "unsold and destroyed" to the publisher. In such case neither the author nor the publisher has received any payment for this "stripped book."

WARNER BOOKS EDITION

Cover design by Julia Kushnirsky
Cover photograph by Sygma/Eddie Adams

Warner Books, Inc.
1271 Avenue of the Americas
New York, NY 10020

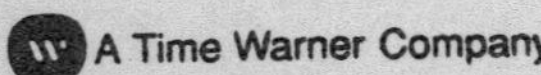

Printed in the United States of America

First Printing: June, 1992

10 9 8 7 6 5 4 3 2 1

The Author

Tony Chiu has been a New York-based journalist since 1966. He has written and edited for The New York Times, People and Life.

In addition, he has published three works of fiction, which include the 1992 deep-sea technothriller "Bright Shark," co-written with the oceanographer/explorer Bob Ballard.

Chiu was born in Shanghai and currently lives in Manhattan, where he is at work on his next novel.

❑

Novels by Tony Chiu

"Bright Shark," with Robert D. Ballard
"Realm Seven"
"Port Arthur Chicken"

CONTENTS

'92's Maverick and Me

Fully half of today's Americans were as yet unborn when Ross Perot last ran for office. The campaign was for the presidency of his senior class at the U.S. Naval Academy. The diminuitive (5'6") Middie, with hair cropped closer than a putting green and wind-flapping ears that could prop up a 20-gallon hat, won and was invited to the White House to shake the hand of his commander-in-chief, the recently inaugurated Dwight D. Eisenhower.

That was precisely four decades ago. Today Mr. Perot is no taller. His hair is grayer but not much longer, his ears still jugged. The only dramatic change is in his financial comfort; since getting in on ground zero of the computer revolution at the end of Eisenhower's second term, the son of a Texarkana, Texas cotton trader has built a net worth hovering around $3 billion, give or take.

Mr. Perot, a proponent of activism, has backed causes from inner-city schools to high culture to international adventures like sending a commando team to rescue employees imprisoned in

Iran. He is no stranger to the corridors of American power. But he has not run for office since leaving Annapolis.

Until now.

On February 20, 1992, Mr. Perot said that if voters would start petition drives to ensure him a spot on the ballots of all 50 states come Election Day, he would run as an independent candidate for the presidency of the United States.

Tellingly, in this age of electronics, his forum was not the front lawn of his boyhood home or some flag-draped podium; it was on CNN cable's talk show, "Larry King Live."

Despite Mr. Perot's small (by major network standards) audience, despite his lack of public profile at the time, despite his rapid-fire East Texas twang, and despite a chuckle that Texas journalist Molly Ivins has compared to a chihuahua's, no one laughed.

For in promising to wage a "first-class" campaign should the petition drives succeed, Mr. Perot said, he would commit in the neighborhood of $100 million. Consider the fact that just two years earlier, such a sum would have paid for the entire national advertising budget—all television, radio and print—of Pepsi, with enough left over to pick up a quarter of Nike's bill that year. And consider what a concerted television campaign did for the visibility of another bulldog-tough private-sector CEO, Chrysler's Lee Iacocca.

But the problem of name recognition quickly receded, and it didn't cost Mr. Perot a penny. He began notching enough magazine covers, newspaper profiles and TV talk-show appearances to turn Hollywood's biggest stars green.

One gauge of Mr. Perot's sudden impact on the national consciousness: the May 9th broadcast of NBC's "Saturday Night Live." The show opened with a Ross Perot impersonator trying to negotiate the presidency with the American public. If he can't raise the national growth rate by at least three percent, he'll waive his $200,000-a-year salary; but beyond three percent, he's entitled to a piece of the profits—with escalation clauses, yet. To show his good faith, he held up a personal check, in the amount of $712 million, to rebuild riot-devastated Los Angeles: "Everything's covered. Done deal. It's over. What I'm saying is that South Central L.A. ... problem solved."

Mr. Perot was skewered with a lighter touch by "SNL" star Dana Carvey than George Bush, who in a hilarious but mean-spirited send-up only three months earlier had been shown endlessly gurgitating and regurgitating his food at a state dinner in Tokyo.

Yet all this intensive media exposure did not begin to answer a key question: Who Is Henry Ross Perot?

A modern-day Cincinnatus, the 5th Century B.C. farmer who twice answered the call to defend his embattled Rome?

Or a higher-tech version of the Wizard of Oz?

In any event, 1992 appeared to be shaping up as one of those times when Americans rediscovered that they're not in Kansas any more—when many were feeling the gnawing dissatisfaction that allows for the possibility of a candidacy by someone beyond the grasp of the two major political parties.

The year following the Soviet disunion and the tumultuous homecoming parades for the Desert Storm veterans had not gone smoothly. The economy had been unable to bounce out of its recession. The national debt kept climbing. And a number of incidents, most of them unplanned, received the kind of saturation, in-your-living-room coverage that guaranteed further cleavages along the thinly-papered fault lines that divide America by economic class, race and gender:

The exposure of fiscal follies within Washington's Beltway that ranged from White House officials using government jets for pleasure to the bad-check artists in Congress;

The perceived judicial wrist-slaps given those convicted of white-collar crimes;

The videotaped mauling of black motorist Rodney King by white Los Angeles cops;

The confirmation hearings on the appointment of Clarence Thomas to the Supreme Court, which triggered accusations of sexual harassment by Oklahoma law professor Anita Hill, as well as her subsequent grilling by the Senate Judiciary Committee;

The outcome of the William Smith Kennedy rape trial, in contrast to that of the Mike Tyson rape trial.

America's disaffection was reflected in its attitudes toward the upcoming presidential elections. The Republican nominee for re-election, George Bush, saw his approval ratings sink to a point where conservative TV commentator Pat Buchanan was regularly commanding 20 percent of the GOP primary vote, even in states where he failed to campaign. Governor Bill Clinton of Arkansas moved to an early lead in the Democratic primaries, then held on for dear Hillary while being attacked from all sides on "character issues."

The sour mood of the electorate was perhaps best expressed by Democratic Senator Lloyd

Bentsen of Texas shortly after Governor Clinton was upset in Connecticut.

"If Jerry Brown is the answer," said Senator Bentsen, "it must be a damned peculiar question."

It was into this fractious arena that Mr. Perot threw his Stetson—sort of. His camp's description of the difficulties of securing places on all 50 state ballots was disingenuous. There have been a number of so-called "third-party" candidacies in this century. None has been as successful as George Wallace's run in 1968, but the problem was not in getting into the race. In the most recent general election, for instance, Lenora B. Fulani, heading the New Alliance Party, ran in all 50 states and won 217,200 votes, while Ron Paul of the Libertarian Party drew 431,616 votes in 46 states.

In any event, by late April Mr. Perot's name had already been secured on the ballots of 16 states, and on May 11, his supporters in Texas marched 90 cartons of petitions to the state house in Austin to gain third-party status for their favorite son.

Constitutional scholars were already having a field day placing articles on Op Ed pages across the nation analyzing the ramifications of a strong showing by Mr. Perot in November. Might the race deadlock in the Electoral College and be thrown into the House of Representatives? And since it would be the freshly-elected Representatives who decided the 42nd President of the United States, might that affect individual House races?

Then another unpredicted event intruded itself into the equation. The acquittal in California, by a jury that contained no black members, of the white police officers who had beaten motorist Rodney King in 1991 set off a spate of protests that quickly escalated out of control. By nightfall, sections of South Central Los Angeles were ablaze. The arson and looting continued for days. White House spokesmen initially blamed the civil unrest on the social welfare programs of the 1960s before lapsing into silence.

Small wonder that the political experts seemed baffled by the presidential race to come. Would 1992 be a year of no rules, of no comforting conventional wisdom? Could that most contradictory of concepts—a populist billionaire—actually have a shot at occupying the Oval Office?

As of May 16, when this is being written, Mr. Perot had not formally declared his candidacy. That step was expected in the month of June, quite possibly on the 27th, which is not only his birthday (he'll turn 62), but also the date on which he was sworn in at the Naval Academy; on which he drew his first post-graduation assignment, aboard a destroyer; on which he founded the company that so enriched him, Electronic Data Systems, Inc. of Dallas; and on which he signed the agreement that paved the way for the sale of EDS, in 1984, for some $2.5 billion, to General Motors.

Author, Author

Here, I will break into the first-person to sum up what this book is—and what it is not.

I have tried to create, if you will, a definitive sourcebook on Ross Perot, one that will illuminate his previous positions and furnish clues to the areas where his public pronouncements are sparse or non-existent.

I make no claims for it as biography—it is less than even an instant bio. The main reason: The excerpting of public-record passages from Mr. Perot's words by definition provides little counterweight to his distinctive voice. The quotes that follow represent his unchallenged viewpoints on the signal events in an oft-contentious life, opinions that are on occasion edited and burnished by reflection. Were this a true biography, there would be scores of friends, colleagues and antagonists to interview (surely Roger Smith, former CEO of General Motors, does not regard himself as a "bully," as Mr. Perot averred; surely Mr. Perot's onetime associates at EDS have thoughts to share about their ex-boss and now competitor).

For the raw material for this book, my associates and I have scoured the country—from Texarkana to Manhattan, from Washington, D.C., to Los Angeles—to collect the many, many words Mr. Perot has written or uttered in public. Some are preserved in articles and books; others in the archives of Congressional subcommittees before which he testified; still others on videotapes or in transcripts. From these sources I've drawn out those that help suggest how Mr. Perot's views on a number of issues have either remained consistent or evolved.

I have tried to be meticulous in excerpting his words so that they remain true to their original context. A citation is provided for each quote and, when necessary, a brief set-up. I have also tried to suggest, by way of my italicized commentary, those events and occasions which other participants may well remember differently. Still, as the master director Akira Kurosawa's classic "Rashomon" teaches us, there may be more truths to an event than all of those who observed it can supply.

Friends who were aware that I've immersed myself in Mr. Perot's public record for nearly three weeks—19 hours at a stretch—have called to ask how I will vote. That answer will be recorded on November 3, in the gymnasium of P.S. 163 on Manhattan's Upper West Side, behind the curtains of the second booth to the right.

By then, Mr. Perot will have experienced at least as many great adventures as Bill and Ted. However he fares, there are two things of which I feel confident.

He is not a Stealth candidate who has left no footprints.

And he will not bore us.

❑

1

From PEA-row To p'ROE

❑

"Never once in my life have I referred to myself as H. Ross Perot.

"I think H. Ross sounds ostentatious and now a huge part of the population thinks I call myself H. Ross.

"My friends don't call me H. Ross. Even my enemies don't call me that."

Wall Street Journal • *August 18, 1988*

❑

"I'm 'Old Ross.' 'Big Ross' is my son."

CNN's "Inside Business" • *January 5, 1992*

❑

"Fortune magazine named me H. Ross Perot in November of 1968."

C-SPAN • *March 18, 1992*

Fortune magazine also named him "The Fastest, Richest Texan" because earlier that year Perot's net worth had zoomed from five digits to nine in the months immediately after EDS, his start-up data processing company, went public.

Thirty-eight years earlier, Gabriel Ross Perot and his wife, Lulu May, had christened their second son Henry Ray. The middle name of Ross, given earlier to Gabriel Jr., who had died of spinal meningitis, was later passed on to Henry. Neither name was used at home; Henry's parents and his older sister, Bette, called him "Brother."

Perot was born in Texarkana, a city that straddles the Texas-Arkansas border. He grew up during the depth of the Depression at 2901 Olive Street in a home built by his cotton-broker father, for $4,400, on the Lone Star side of the state line.

❑

"We lived about six blocks from the railroad tracks, and the tramps would jump off the trains and come up to our house, looking for food. They were really dirty and tough-looking, but my mother would feed them. People showed up every day, and she never turned anybody away. One day a man came by and said, 'Lady, do a lot of people come through here looking for food?' And she said, 'Yes.' And he said, 'Don't you know why?' And she said, 'No.' And he said, 'You're a mark.' He showed her where the tramps had made a mark on the curb in front of our house. That was a sign to other tramps that they would be fed there. After the man left, I said, 'Mother, do you want me to wipe that off?' And she said, 'No, leave it there. Those people are just like you and me. The difference is, they're down on their luck.'"

Dallas Times Herald • *February 9, 1986*

❑

"My business success stems mainly from having sat in my dad's cotton brokerage office, watching him build trust and confidence among the farmers. After a while he started letting me trade horses and cattle. I had to buy and sell the same day. 'You don't take 'em home,' he said, 'because then you've got to feed 'em.' Under his tutelage I really learned how to negotiate."

Life • *February 1988*

Although one boyhood chum fondly remembered pranks like transplanting a "Men At Work" sign from a construction site to the front lawn of the class beauty, Perot was a serious entrepreneur from early on. Joining the Flaming Arrow Patrol at 11, he made Eagle Scout in just 18 months. In addition, he sold everything from magazines to seeds door-to-door; delivered papers in the poor, predominantly black Newtown sec-

tion; and in his spare time broke broncos for $1.50 a head.

❑

"I threw newspapers to whorehouses. I knew all the women. I threw them the paper, and they paid me on time. I threw papers to flop houses to some of the poorest people in the world. They tried to hold me up every Sunday. I was on horseback, and the animal would sense people, so they never ever got close. But they weren't bad people. They were desperate."

The Dallas Morning News • June 29, 1986

❑

"I was thrown [from broncos] a lot. That's how I broke my nose. And I don't know how many concussions I got.

"After a while, I figured out a way to break a horse without getting knocked out. I would tie up one of his legs with a rag and make him stand on three legs. In five minutes he would be exhausted and trembling. Then I could untie his leg and ride him as long as I wanted to. I didn't get bucked off anymore, so I wasn't always recovering from some injury, and I could ride more horses than before. The more horses I rode, the more money I made."

Dallas Times Herald • February 9, 1986

❑

"I grew up in a home where you were expected to do what you are supposed to do. You could probably cut a lot of other stuff out and leave it right there."

Dallas Times Herald • September 4, 1983

❑

"One year my father sold one of his horses in order to have enough money for Christmas presents and Christmas dinner. That really bothered me because I knew how much he loved that horse. But it also showed us how much he loved us."

The Washington Post • April 12, 1987

❑

"If you had stopped me and said, 'Son, what do you want to do when you grow up?' I'm sure I would have said I want to get enough education so I can work indoors. I know that much."

Todd Gold's "Perot: An Unauthorized Biography"

❑

"You ever see that movie 'Places in the Heart?' That's the town I knew."

The Washington Post • April 12, 1987

Perot was not to leave his hometown immediately. He spent two years studying pre-law at Texarkana Junior College, where he was elected senior class president, before winning an appointment to the United States Naval Academy. He was sworn in on his 19th birthday, June 27, 1949.

❑

Sailing, Sailing

At Annapolis, Perot had to get used to a new pronunciation of his surname (instructors and classmates alike ignored the East Texas PEA-row, preferring the p'ROE of his French forebears) as well as a heavy academic workload.

"I'd have to say that I was an average student, subject to very difficult subjects. I really didn't have the background or preparations for those [predominantly engineering] subjects."

D Magazine • January, 1984

Academically he finished No. 454 in a graduating class of 925. Perot was more successful outside the classroom; said his yearbook: "What Ross lacked in physical size, he more than adequately replaced by his capacity to make friends and influence people." In fact, he won the presidency of his junior and senior classes as well as the lifetime presidency of the Annapolis Class of '53.

On June 27 of that year, the freshly-minted ensign shipped out on the Sigourney. Before the destroyer could take up station off Korea, an armistice was declared; the ship ended up on an extended around-the-world cruise.

"When you go to sea for a year, that's like 10 years of short cruises. There were 300 of us on board. We were together in cramped quarters 24 hours a day, and we were at sea for six and seven weeks at a time. That's the best practical experience in management and leadership that I could have gotten anywhere in the world. And it was a heck of a trip for a kid who had never been anywhere but Fort Worth—17 seas and oceans, 24 countries."

Dallas Times Herald • February 9, 1986

At sea, Perot worked with some of the ship's computers.

"In the land of the blind, the one-eyed man is king. I had touched a computer at a time when very few people had."

The Dallas Morning News • June 29, 1986

Thus, when he met an IBM executive fulfilling his naval reserve obligation aboard the carrier Leyte, the two struck up a conversation. By that time, Perot had begun to chafe under both the command of a particular superior and the Navy's lock-step system of promotion.

In 1957, after four years of service and a successful job interview with IBM, Lieut. Perot left the Navy. (Though the Navy never left him: In the mid-1970s, on the eve of the Middies' annual football showdown with Army, he was caught inside the West Point chapel banging out "Anchors Aweigh" on the chimes.) He and his new bride, Margot Birmingham, a Goucher grad from western Pennsylvania whom he'd met on a blind date, drove their Plymouth cross-country to Dallas, where Perot began selling computers.

❑

"Things were so good in those days at IBM that a salesman could get rich as long as he didn't get drunk during the day. It didn't take a miracle worker to get somewhere."

The Washington Post • April 12, 1987

Perot worked on commission. When he began to take home more than his supervisor, he accepted a cut in commissions just to stay busy. Still, in 1962, he sold his year's quota on January 19 and began to contemplate the boring 49 weeks that lay ahead.

"If I'd stayed at IBM, I'd be somewhere in middle management getting in trouble and being asked to take early retirement. When I got up to the bite-your-tongue level, that's when I would have gotten in trouble."

The Washington Post, April 12, 1987

❑

"One day I was in the barber shop waiting to have my hair cut, looking at an old Reader's Digest. At the end of the stories they have these little one-liners, and they had Thoreau's quote, 'The mass of men lead lives of quiet desperation.' And I said, 'There I am,' I said, 'I'm going to try this or I'll never be able to live with myself.'"

ABC's "20/20" • April 3, 1986

A Company With Byte

"This" was a concept he'd been unable to get off the ground within IBM. In those days, there was no off-the-shelf software. As a result, the company sold the

hardware, then helped clients cobble together the necessary programming and trained their operators. Perot had proposed establishing a service division to take over data storage and retrieval.

Though lacking the resources to purchase a computer, Perot knew that most mainframes sat idle from 5 p.m. to 9 a.m. and all weekend long. He thought he could lease this dead time from IBM's clients and form a company to specialize in data processing.

On June 27, 1962—his 32nd birthday—he borrowed $1,000 of the savings Margot had accumulated as a teacher and incorporated Electronic Data Systems, Inc., a grand name for a firm with one employee and a $100-a-month lease on a one-room office.

But Perot had a well-grounded vision that started with a certain type of employee, which he described to a New York-based reporter in 1968: "We aren't looking for just the needle in the hay stack. We're looking for the needle with the red dot on it."

The recruits who joined a nucleus of Perot's ex-IBM colleagues tended to be fellow ex-servicemen who thrived under the pressure of night and weekend work and who seemed not to mind EDS's no-frills atmosphere. Marital fidelity was a must, as Perot told the author of a March, 1974, profile in The Plain Truth (published by radio evangelist Garner Ted Armstrong's Ambassador College and Worldwide Church of God), as were no-martini lunches.

❑

"If we have a married employee who has a girl friend, we terminate him. He's got a lifetime contract with his wife, and if she can't trust him, how can I? It's that simple."

Dallas Times Herald • March 14, 1974

❑

"I haven't sold anybody over lunch in my whole life. There's nothing worse than driving home a point when a guy's fiddling with his salad."

Look • March 24, 1970

❑

Hair on faces and over the collar was banned.

"I am frequently asked, you know, what I think of young people with long hair. I have to be very careful there, because I have an extreme haircut, too. You know, it is a matter of personalities."

ABC's "Issues and Answers" • January 11, 1970

EDSers were also expected to be conservative of mien. Women were forbidden to wear slacks except in deep winter, and the men were given a dress code, Perot said, because many Vietnam veterans were being hired.

"They had no civilian clothes. We'd hire 'em and tell 'em to wear business suits. Well, these guys would come back with the worst looking combinations you've ever seen... so somebody wrote a little outline of the kind of stuff they needed to buy."

The Dallas Morning News • July 6, 1986

❑

"How much confidence would a bank or other client have in EDS if a representative of the company showed up in his office in jeans and a mop of uncut hair?"

New York Daily News • February 22, 1970

❑

In early 1979, though, the boss chose to overlook an EDSer's mustache, probably because Perot visited him in Tehran's Gasr Prison, where the man was a hostage of the Iranian authorities:

"Keep it. Anyway, we're going to change the dress code. We've had the results of the employee attitude survey, and we'll probably permit mustaches, and colored shirts, too."

EDSer: "And beards?"

Perot: "No beards."

Ken Follett's "On Wings of Eagles"

❑

"It's informal here. Anybody can come see me at any time. Everyone here can call me Ross. That is hardly a Nazi youth camp. What gets under my skin? Anybody who says anyone who works out here is a clone. Everybody around here has a very high regard for his own opinion."

The Dallas Morning News • June 28, 1981

❑

EDS's first major account, Frito-Lay, then a Dallas-based snack company, was billed $5,128 per month for data processing:

"I used odd numbers like $5,128 in those days to make it look like I knew exactly what I was doing and had figured everything down to the last penny.

"And I would say, 'We want you to pay us in advance.' And they would say, 'Why?' And I would say, 'Well, that's customary in the computer business.' In fact, if they hadn't paid me in advance, I couldn't have paid my people. That's the blocking and tackling that started EDS. It was a great adventure and a lot of fun. And I wouldn't want to do it again."

Dallas Times Herald • February 9, 1986

In 1965, business was still slow enough that Perot worked part-time for Blue Cross and Blue Shield of Texas. That year Congress enacted Medicare—mandating that each state handle its own claims—and thus guaranteed the success of EDS.

Starting with a successful bid to computerize Texas' program, Perot quickly branched out to other states until his firm was reporting $1.5 million-a-year profits.

Yet Perot kept the purse strings drawn tight. His office was decorated with tag-sale prints of a clipper ship and of an Indian, gun in hand, leaning against a telephone pole and staring at the horizon. "I like what I like, not because it's worth something," he proudly told one reporter, "No picture in my office is worth more than $25."

In 1968, Wall Street came a-courting. When EDS went public, Perot, who held roughly 90 percent of the shares, suddenly found himself a millionaire 205 times over, not to mention the subject of that admiring "H. Ross" profile in Fortune. Other writers soon copied, for Perot was supremely opinionated and compulsively quotable.

❑

"When your men go up every day against IBM, you build a lean, hard company.

"There's a greater body of knowledge in EDS

on how to effectively use a computer in a commercial company than in any other company in the world. And that includes IBM."

Business Week • *August 30, 1969*

❑

"We're a technical company. But you can't run a technical company with technicians. You've got to run it with businessmen."

The Dallas Morning News • *May 3, 1970*

❑

"The words 'management' and 'labor' create divisions among people. And if my team is eaten up with internal politics, infighting, backbiting and what have you, and you bring in a unified team... you're going to beat me every time."

Newsweek • *June 17, 1985*

❑

"I'm all for unions, but we don't need 'em. There's a sign over the gate of Toyota City [in Japan] and it says, 'Every worker is a brother.' That's EDS."

The Washington Post • *April 12, 1987*

❑

On why he didn't like to receive memos:
"I want a live, breathing human being in here saying, 'Look, I think you ought to do this, and here's why.'"

Inc. • *January, 1989*

❑

"Brains and wits will beat capital all the time. There is a tendency in big corporations to rely too much on capital. [EDS] beat IBM without any capital."

Wall Street Journal • *July 22, 1986*

❑

"We don't like government business. We don't do any business direct with the government. Because to the government a horse is an animal with four legs, a head, and a tail, whether it's a jack-ass or a race horse."

The Dallas Morning News • *May 3, 1970*

EDS—at this time primarily a government subcontractor—continued to grow like a mushroom in a spring rain. The firm's 300 employees in 1968 swelled to 1,800 in 1970, a headcount that almost doubled again in the next year. Revenues kept apace. Perot *began to win local attention for both his new riches—and the manner in which he gave away large dollops of it, including $2.5 million for a pilot elementary school in the black ghettos of South Dallas.*

❑

"I know what the stereotype is, if you're rich and from Dallas, everybody expects you to be far right. I say look at what I've done and it isn't so."

The Washington Post • November 23, 1969

❑

In late 1969, his celebrity went national when he announced plans to fly two cargo jets laden with medical supplies and food to Southeast Asia. Perot's goal: distributing the relief to an estimated 1,400 American POWs being held in North Vietnam.

"This is not a campaign to support Mr. Nixon himself—it was to support the office he holds.

"If Hubert Humphrey were President today, I'd be standing behind him."

The New York Times • November 28, 1969

❑

On who was behind his POW crusade:
"I'm like the door-to-door salesman who knocked on my door and asked if he could come in. I asked whom he was with. He said, 'I'm not with anybody. I'm by myself.'"

New York Daily News • February 22, 1970

❑

"We told the government if we're ever doing anything that is not in the national interest—just whisper it once lightly in our ear and we'll stop."

The Dallas Morning News • February 19, 1973

That mission (discussed more fully in Chapter Two: "Crusader or Quixote?") was ultimately denied landing privileges by an understandably suspicious Hanoi, but it further ingratiated Perot with the highest levels of Richard Nixon's first administration (to which the Texan had been a heavyweight campaign donor).

"Back in the days before they put a lid on campaign contributions, everybody that ran for president came into my office and twisted my arm. In 1968, every candidate except the guy who ran from the Communist Party came in here figuring, 'Here's a place where we can squeeze.' When they were investigating Nixon [during Watergate], the FBI called down and said, 'Did [Nixon finance chairman] Maurice Stans come see you?' I said, 'Yeah.' They said, 'Did he put pressure on you?' And I said, 'Compared to whom? Maurice Stans was a pussycat compared to the rest of these guys.'"

D Magazine • January, 1984

❑

"Well, for 37/39ths of my life, I've been on the other side. Two years ago, I couldn't find the door to the Establishment. No, I don't consider myself a member of the Establishment and I don't want to become a member.

"A large bank asked me to become a board member the other day but I declined. I knew they had asked me not from my knowledge of banks but because of my bank deposits."

The Dallas Morning News • January 11, 1970

Three months later, on April 22, 1970, Perot suddenly found himself with a lot less to deposit. Without warning, EDS stock went into freefall. By the end of the day, Perot was out an astonishing $450 million—until Black Monday in October of 1987, his was the largest loss ever suffered by a single investor. The silver lining: he had $1 billion left.

❑

"People asked me what I felt. Money is strange. I felt sorry for the little investors who got taken to the cleaners. But what did I feel for myself? I felt nothing."

The Washington Post • April 12, 1987

❑

Later that year, the leftist magazine Ramparts tried to take the Texan himself to the cleaners. Its 10-page exposé of EDS's growing portfolio of profitable social services contracts was headlined, "H. Ross Perot: America's First Welfare Billionaire." Writer Robert Fitch was hardly a neutral observer, as witness this passage: "In a rambling two-hour interview carried out in his gigantic executive office, furnished in American motel, Perot shrugged off all the hostile criticism of EDS's California operation." The writer seemed unimpressed that Perot granted him two hours.

Fitch accused EDS of a dismal record in minority hiring, and of purging blacks on the staff of California Blue Shield when it won the contract to provide computer services to CBS.

But Perot was allowed to rebut the charge that EDS was acting improperly by refusing to open its books to the government.

"IBM is the world's largest natural monopoly. It's selling millions of dollars of computer hardware to California. And it doesn't have to tell the state what its costs are."

Ramparts • November, 1970

Wild, Wild East

As the American economy labored under the strain of the seemingly endless Vietnam War, the financial markets which had so battered Perot's fortunes continued showing signs of acute distress. In Washington, some of the president's men rightly figured that the Texan not only retained deep pockets, but also savored challenges. They asked him to shore up the finances of the major Wall Street brokerage house of F.I. duPont Glore Forgan, for which EDS had recently contracted to run back-office operations. The ante: $5 million.

Perot, who in late 1972 joined McDonald's founder Ray Kroc and nine others in receiving a Horatio Alger Award (to those who "overcame humble beginnings to earn acclaim in their professions"), readily agreed and laid plans to take Manhattan.

❑

"The typical broker is trained that you're an independent businessman, that you've got your own operation out here within our company, that you can make a tremendous amount of money in a very short period of time. The whole presentation to you to come into brokerage is how much you can make how soon. Nobody ever talks about making money for the customer.

"We've done a lot of studies since we made our investment in duPont. And it just roars out at you from these studies that the investor feels that he's not been fairly dealt with.

"We are hiring men at the rate of 50 men a month. I don't want anybody that has any brokerage experience. We want to vaccinate these fellows a different way. We want to train them to make money for their clients.

"Our brokers are going to be putting their clients' money away in many cases. See, there's a concept—most of your money ought to be put in long-term situations.

"As we tell our fellows in our school, if the [client] wants to shoot dice, tell him to get two brokers. He can get a broker down the street to shoot dice with."

The Dallas Morning News • *October 15, 1972*

❑

On the gung-ho EDS spirit he was trying to foster with signs like "The cowards never started, the weak died on the way... only the strong survived":

"It's like a cold shower. You're either attracted by it or repelled by it. If you don't like it, there are a lot of other opportunities."

The New York Times • September 10, 1971

❑

"You know, a lady once came up to me and said, 'Perot, if you were a member of a minority group, you'd know how tough things are.' I said: 'Lady, if you think I'm not a member of a minority group, you try being a Texan on Wall Street.'

"It was at this time that I got rid of my cowboy boots and Roy Rogers suits."

Los Angeles Times • November 10, 1972

❑

"[Major houses] remind me of a trip through the Suez Canal. Ever been there? Every morning, as the sun rises across the desert, the banks of the canal are swarming with natives dipping sand out of the canal and hauling it in buckets out into the desert. That night, the wind blows it back into the canal and the next morning they are back repeating their task."

Business Week • May 26, 1973

❑

On himself, in a newspaper ad for duPont (one of the few times he has tooted his own horn):
"For 38 years of my life I was a 'little guy.' There are so many of us. We are America. We make this big engine go. That's why duPont is interested in the individual investor."

Time • June 4, 1973

❑

On the very need for a stock exchange:
"A broker called one of his clients and said, 'I have a great opportunity for $2 a share.'

"'Buy a thousand shares,' said his client.

"The broker called back and said, 'I have a great opportunity at $5 a share in the same company.'

"'Buy me a thousand shares.'

"This kept up until he got to $55 a share. Then he called his broker and said, 'Sell.' There was silence on the other end of the phone. Finally the broker said, 'To whom?'

"That man was the whole market in that situation. The function of the New York Stock Exchange is to provide the 'To Whom.'"

Testimony before the House Committee on Ways and Means • March 21, 1973

Perot may have grasped the mechanics, but not the market, which continued bearish. In January of 1974, his firm, having become one of the Top 3 by way of merger to become duPont Walston & Co., closed its 143 branches, pink-slipped its 2,000 salesmen and bade farewell to its 300,000 customers. His charge through the canyons of New York's financial district cost Perot an estimated $60 million.

❑

A decade and a half later, Perot had rationalized his own part in the duPont fiasco. Basically, he felt he had been snookered:

"I was encouraged by virtually everybody at a senior level in government in Washington, and certainly by everybody at a senior level in Wall Street, and certainly by everybody running a major New York bank, to step in to avoid what they perceived to be an impending disaster, because there was no specific legislation to bail out a failing firm. Keep in mind Chrysler and Lockheed had not yet occurred. Since [the Securities Investor Protection Corporation] didn't exist then, the New York Stock Exchange at that time was responsible for taking over the firms that had failed, and had a fund to do that. But it was broke. And now a major firm, duPont Glore Forgan, was going under, and the story was that the market would stop.

"See, we believed the story that the stock market would stop trading. Now, I don't blame anybody except myself. I was grown.

"I didn't have any problem with Wall Street. I was trying to farm when there wasn't any rain."

Barron's • February 23, 1987

A Talon for the Game

Perot returned to Dallas and to EDS. The company had flourished under the day-to-day leadership of able lieutenants, and they continued to oversee operations—unless an emergency arose.

Christmasing with his family at their Vail ski chalet in late December of 1978, Perot received a call that two EDS executives had been jailed in Iran.

The company was under contract to computerize that nation's social security accounts. But as the Shah's dictatorial regime wavered under increasing pressure from followers of the exiled fundamentalist Ayatollah Khomeini, Tehran had suspended its payments. In return, EDS had evacuated most of its employees. Now, the Iranian government had seized two of the remaining Americans and was demanding almost $13 million for their release.

When Perot's calls to Washington brought no satis-

faction, he contacted retired Army Ranger Arthur "Bull" Simons, commander of a legendary raid in the early 1970s on a North Vietnamese prison camp to search for American POWs. Simons agreed to lead a volunteer team of Vietnam-tested EDSers into Tehran in hopes of springing their colleagues.

Perot decided to go to Iran in a last-ditch attempt to negotiate his men's release before Simons launched his mission. He arrived at Mehrabad Airport in strife-ridden Tehran on January 13, 1979.

❑

On how a Texas billionaire managed to slip through immigration control posing as an NBC-TV courier:
"They weren't looking for an ugly American."

Ken Follett's "On Wings of Eagles"

Perot left Iran several days later, before the mission began. Through much pluck—and even more luck, by way of a providential anti-Shah riot—the Simons team pulled off the jailbreak and escaped into Turkey, where an anxious Perot was one of their greeters.

❑

On accepting the Distinguished Texan Award 18 months after the Tehran rescue:
"I think... that it is somewhat ironic that if the rescue hadn't worked, I would have been portrayed

as an idiot for having tried it, irresponsible for having gotten some of our people killed, and I would have been in prison and you sure as hell wouldn't be giving me an award."

The Dallas Morning News • September 25, 1980

❑

On his epitaph, circa 1980:

"Made more money faster. Lost more money in one day. Led the biggest jailbreak in history. He died.

"Footnote: The New York Times questioned whether he really did the jailbreak or not."

The Dallas Morning News • June 28, 1981

The Iranian adventure was recounted in Ken Follett's 1983 book, "On Wings of Eagles," the text of which was subject to Perot's approval.

"Ken [Follett] would ask me to read drafts of the book. When he got to the fourth draft, he bet me a Rolls-Royce that I couldn't find any errors. I found two. I said, 'It's Admiral Mountbatten, not General. And you spelled McDonald's wrong.'

"A couple weeks later, a Rolls-Royce arrived—on a key chain. Ken said, 'I didn't say what size you'd get.'"

New York Post • April 27, 1986

The success of the Follett book led to a five-hour NBC mini-series by the same name, over which Perot also had final approval.

❑

On vetoing, for the role of mission leader Simons, actor Robert Preston:

"I remembered him as 'The Music Man.' Colonel Simons is not a Music Man."

The Dallas Morning News • May 18, 1986

❑

On the (much taller) actor he approved to portray Perot:

"There are a few details in the show that aren't accurate, and probably the ultimate fiction is the casting of Richard Crenna as me. His acting was right on the money, but he's much better looking than I am and speaks much better than I do. A lot of guys at EDS have given me a hard time. They tell me Mickey Rooney would have been more appropriate casting."

The New York Times • May 5, 1986

❑

"I'm not a living legend. I'm just a myth."

Todd Gold's "Perot: An Unauthorized Biography"

❑

The year after the Tehran rescue, Perot was vacationing with Margot and their five children during the final stages of the competition for Texas' Medicare account. Though EDS had been prime contractor for 13 years, the new assignment was awarded to a New York company. Perot immediately jetted home to field-marshal a counterattack that eventually swung the account back to EDS. One source quoted in the January, 1989, issue of Inc. magazine said, "It was Perot as classic SOB. He came screaming out of the sky, talons bared, and ripped their eyes out."

"What is an EDSer? An EDSer is a person who goes anywhere, anytime, 24 hours a day, seven days a week, to make sure that EDS is the finest computer company in the world and that nobody beats us in competition."

Texas Monthly • December, 1988

❑

"We published a book on how to be president of EDS, how to get to the top. I can assure you it's carefully read."

Dallas Times Herald • August 21, 1984

One excerpt from that 1984 booklet:

"First, there are no geniuses in this group. In terms of mental capacity, they would probably be ranked slightly above average. One characteristic stands out. These people are honest. They do what they say they will do. This causes other people to trust them. This creates an opportunity for these people to lead. Never forget, trust is fragile. It takes years to earn. It can be lost in an instant. It must be re-earned each time you have contact with another person."

❑

By the end of 1980, though, the company Perot had founded in a $100-a-month office was no longer a messianic start-up, but a bigfoot in the rapidly-maturing computer services industry. Many of EDS's original staff had survived the long march, but the firm had grown so large that he no longer personally knew most of its employees.

On having turned 51:

"I'm excess baggage on this company now. I could shake hands with everyone today and never come back, and you would never see the difference."

The Dallas Morning News • June 28, 1981

On the livestock that grazed the grounds of EDS's campus-like headquarters in north Dallas.

"You can see our buffalo and longhorns. I don't have much use for 'em but I sure love to go look at 'em."

The Washington Post • April 12, 1987

By this time, the Perot Foundation was well established. Run by his older sister Bette, the charity was distributing an average of $5 million a year, concentrating on social services like education, shelters and abused-spouse centers.

❑

"My biggest problem in giving money for social programs is finding somebody who can use it intelligently."

The New York Times • April 28, 1970

❑

On philanthropy:

"It's a difficult thing to do it and do it well. It's actually harder to give it away intelligently than it is to make it."

The Dallas Morning News • June 28, 1981

❑

Perot's donations also benefited local attractions like the Dallas Arboretum and the Morton H. Meyerson Symphony Center (named for an ex-EDS president) and what other eclectic causes caught his eye. These included the New York P. D. (he gave its mounted patrol 20 purebred Tennessee walking horses); Dr. Elizabeth Morgan, the Washington, D.C., plastic surgeon jailed for more than two years after refusing to surrender her daughter to her ex-husband, dentist Eric Foretich, whom she accused of child abuse; Austin's famed 500-year-old Treaty Oak after it was poisoned with pesticides; and an Army PFC from Idaho severely wounded during Desert Storm.

On purchasing for the University of Texas a $15 million rare-book collection that included Shakespeare folios:

"What does a guy who was trained as a sailor and worked all his life in high tech know about great books? Not much."

U.S. News & World Report • February 3, 1986

❑

On buying one of four surviving copies of the Magna Carta in 1985, for $1.5 million:

"My lawyer found it for me in England. When he was getting ready to come home with it, he asked me if I wanted security guards on it and all that. I said, 'Hell, stick it in your briefcase.' When he was at Heathrow [Airport in London], one of the guards said, 'What have you got there?' Tom said, 'The Magna Carta.' Guard never missed a beat. He just said, 'That's very well. Have a nice flight.'"

The Washington Post • April 12, 1987

In the early 1980s, the man who thrived on solving problems went outside EDS to take on two of the largest that faced Texas: drugs and public school reform (discussed more fully in Chapter Two: "Crusader or Quixote?").

Perot was winding down his public-sector service when, on April 2, 1984, the phone rang.

Roger and Me

That year, the rising tide of Reaganomics was lifting a lot of boats—but not the vehicles manufactured by Detroit's automakers. Of the Big Three, General Motors had started the decade under new chairman Roger Smith with the most visionary plans: not only cars for the future, but a new method of production, a vision fit for the 21st Century, that was embodied by the built-from-scratch, $5-billion Saturn plant in Tennessee. Trouble was, America's appetite was continuing to *shift from Detroit Iron to cars from Japan, perceived as boasting better engineering, better values and better quality control.*

For a number of reasons (capably set out in Doron P. Levin's 1989 "Irreconcilable Differences"), Smith was interested in adding EDS to the GM family; at the very least, he thought the formidable computer skills of Perot's company could help cohere the far-flung General Motors empire.

The phone call to Perot came from a New York investment banker representing GM.

Perot was astonished by the overture. But with EDS having reached a point where ever larger contracts were needed to maintain growth, giant GM represented the ultimate client. In addition, since the automaker used so many contractors, an affiliation might open the doors to future work outside of GM. Perot, backed by his top advisors, agreed to exploratory meetings.

❑

On inviting a high-powered Manhattan attorney to a business lunch in Dallas:

"I took him to Johnny's Barbeque. Now Johnny ran a beautiful place, but this day we had it looking bad, like you wouldn't slow down to feed your cat.

"We walked in, and [the lawyer] asked, 'Is this

your club?' I said, 'Oh, yes, this is the kind of club we have in Texas.

"Johnny was wearing a greasy apron and a greasy hat, and he was wiping the counter with a greasy cloth. He leaned over to this guy and said, 'How d'ya want your armadillo?' The lawyer thought for a minute and then he said, 'Well done, I suppose.'

"He ate a whole plate of beef, thinking it was armadillo, and he said it was great."

The Dallas Morning News • June 29, 1986

❑

On his initial face-to-face session with Smith:

"I told Roger at the end of the first day, 'Roger, you don't have to buy a dairy to get the milk... We'll sell you the service.'"

The Washington Post • July 7, 1985

❑

But General Motors wanted the whole herd. After an intense three-month courtship, on June 27, 1984—Perot's 54th birthday—he signed a memorandum of understanding that agreed to GM's $2.5 billion acquisition of EDS. It was a complicated transaction that *bestowed on him 11.3 million shares (or about one percent) of GM stock, worth some $1.5 billion at the time, and a seat on the board.*

By this time, Perot was hoping to use his position as GM's largest shareholder to help the company revitalize itself. Such a task seemed a perfect fit in light of his historic concerns, grown sharper of late, about American competitiveness. Perhaps GM, one of the most conspicuous examples of muscle-bound bureaucracy, could become a textbook case of returning to earlier values.

It was in that spirit that Perot had a 1945 Norman Rockwell painting, "Homecoming Marine," hung in the anteroom of his Dallas office.

"The Marine is there to remind my GM visitors that we used to whip the Japanese right regularly. And if we ever decide we want to do it again in the car business, we can."

Business Week • October 6, 1986

As Levin describes in "Irreconcilable Differences," it was not a marriage made in corporate heaven. The GM and EDS staffs clashed bitterly over matters as diverse as the pay scale for Perot lieutenants and the mark-ups EDS took for providing its new siblings with computer services. Nor did it help the meshing of cultures when GMers openly referred to EDSers as "cor-

porate Moonies" and "Perot-bots." The following year, Perot lost his fight to block GM's $5.2-billion buyout of Hughes Aircraft. He had also become frustrated by his inability to exert influence on either top management or the board (some members of whom, The Wall Street Journal reported, "Mr. Perot privately referred to... as 'old farts' and 'pet rocks'").

In mid-1986, he declared open season on General Motors.

❑

"It takes five years to develop a new car in this country. Heck, we won World War II in four years. We are spending billions to develop new cars. This isn't a moon shot, it's just a car.

"Having slow, orderly, evolutionary change just means that we aren't going to change at all. It's time we stopped talking about making the best cars, it's time to make them. I'm not going to rest until we're shipping cars to Japan."

The Wall Street Journal • July 22, 1986

❑

"Revitalizing GM is like teaching an elephant to tap-dance. You find the sensitive spots and start poking."

Business Week • October 6, 1986

❑

"Let's say there is a problem with the brakes. They will send some bright, highly motivated staff person, probably a financial type, to check on the brake problem. He talks with an accountant who talks to someone in long-range planning, and finally they form a committee to talk to some poor devil working on brakes who knows what the hell to do."

Ward's Auto World • November, 1986

❑

On GM's late-1986 lay-off of 30,000 workers, with plans to terminate 29,000 more and close 11 plants:
"I grew up in a world where good, decent people had it tough and had to look hard for work. For heaven's sake, let's get in the game and get the product so competitive that we don't have to do this again."

The New York Times • November 7, 1986

❑

"I finally found that, not being effective internally, I had to take public positions about the need to get competitive. I understood that they didn't like it, but I tried to make it clear that none of it was personal. One of the GM guys said to me once, 'Why are you so intense?' I said, 'If you had the investment I had, you'd be intense, too.'"

The New York Times • *December 2, 1986*

❑

Dismissing GM's countercharges as the bitter boardroom fight entered its endgame:

"Gorilla dust. When gorillas fight, they throw dust in the air to confuse each other."

Newsweek • *December 15, 1986*

On December 1, 1986, after three weeks of behind-the-scenes negotiations, the gorilla dust settled: General Motors bought back Perot's 11.3 million shares. Though Perot collected roughly $700 million, he had to sever his ties to EDS and its employees, which now numbered 48,000. Further, he could not start a computer data services company that would compete with EDS before June 1, 1988.

One clause in the buyout specified that should Perot henceforth criticize GM—or vice versa—the wounded party was entitled to collect $7.5 million. Within hours, Perot was openly calling his forced departure "hush-mail;" as a gag rule, that clause ranked right up there in effectiveness with the latest Serbo-Croatian armistice.

❑

"GM shot the messenger."

Time • December 15, 1986

❑

"Dissent is obviously considered bad form. Or, to quote a professor from Wharton [School of Business], he said my speaking out was like coming to a board meeting barefoot."

Newsweek • December 15, 1986

One week later, Perot kept a long-standing date to speak in the Motor City. Sharing the dais before an overflow audience with Roger Smith, he refrained from zinging GM directly, but used the occasion to launch a fresh round of thinly-cloaked broadsides against corporate bloat which has abated—somewhat—in the years since.

"If you go to war, you feed the troops before you feed the officers. You can't look the troops in the eye and say, 'It's been a bad year; we can't do anything for you,' but then say, 'By the way, we're going to pay ourselves a $1 million bonus.'"

Speech to the Economic Club of Detroit • December 8, 1986

"You know there's high tech, low tech and no tech. It's been my experience that every GM car leaks oil."

Life • *February 1988*

❑

"I had several memorable experiences with GM. One, it just drove me crazy that when a customer had a problem with a defective engine, we wanted to treat it as a class action suit rather than fix the engine."

CNN's "Inside Business" • *January 5, 1992*

Off Warranty

Perhaps the extent of GM's problems, both in selling cars and its once-proud corporate image, is best summed up by the fact that Perot emerged from the debacle a folk hero of sorts.

In February of 1987, the Dallas Press Club staged a Perot roast.

Tracy Rowlett of WFAA-TV observed that the honoree had just flown in from a business trip, "and boy, are his ears tired."

Former local TV newscaster Murphy Martin added, "As the press knows, he can talk two hours on any sub-

ject and four hours if he knows a little bit about it."

And Gov. Mark White, recently voted out of office, referred obliquely to Perot's $750 million GM package: "We were both asked to leave. I took my lumps and left Austin, and he took his in lumps."

Tributes were nice. But enjoined for 18 months from the business he knew best, Perot found himself, for the first time in his life, no longer drawing a salary (it had been $68,000 per year, the same as when EDS had gone public in 1968).

❑

At a conference of U.S. governors:
"Only in America would a guy who's out of work be invited to explain to 50 governors how to put this country to work."

Dallas Times Herald • February 24, 1987

❑

"Now that I've got all this cash, I've got to figure out what to do with it."

The Washington Post • April 12, 1987

❑

On investing $20 million in Apple co-founder Steve Jobs' new start-up computer company:
"My friends say that NeXT can't die with my ego

and Steve's ego in it. At least it will never fail for lack of money."

Fortune • March 2, 1987

Perot would withdraw from NeXT in June of 1991. By that time, though, he had not only launched another computer services company, Perot Systems, but also begun to directly challenge EDS for contracts. His old firm, which continues to do quite nicely without its founder (1992 headcount: 65,000), has been enmeshed with Perot Systems in a series of bittersweet lawsuits over a variety of matters; by early 1992, an uneasy truce had settled over the battlefield.

Perot also participated in non-Perot Systems projects like Alliance Airport, which Ross Jr. is developing into a cargo-only facility near Dallas-Fort Worth Airport to service a new industrial complex. (Alliance, which is sited on the 13,000 acres of real estate Perot assembled, might become a campaign issue, since its development has been helped by $41 million of Federal aid to date; another $120 million has been requested.)

❑

On his ability to assemble a bloc of property for Alliance Airport:

"The stockyard used to be south of this land and the wind blew the smell north, maybe that's why no one moved there. There's no stockyard there now."

Wall Street Journal • December 2, 1986

The plaque outside the office of the head of Perot Systems reads: "Every good and excellent thing stands moment by moment on the razor's edge of danger, and must be fought for."

Inside, Perot's tag-sale prints have long been replaced by a portrait of George Washington by Gilbert Stuart; Archibald Willard's patriotic 1876 canvas of Revolutionary War fife-and-drummers, "Spirit of '76," signed Norman Rockwells, and Old West bronzes by Frederick Remington. Memorabilia include a crystal-encased rattlesnake head and the weapons belt of a Peoples Republic of China officer "liberated" during an American raid on Hanoi.

❑

"I have filled this office with things I like and with things my wife and four daughters have asked me please not to bring home."

The New York Times, June 11, 1989

Conspicuous by its absence is the office equipment from which Perot's fortunes derived: the computer.

"The computer is just a thing. It cannot see, feel or act until it is first acted on. It can reduce the profusion of dead ends involved in vital research, but it cannot connect a man to the things he must be connected to—the reality of pain in others, the possibility of creative growth within himself, the memory of the human race and the rights of the next generation."

The Dallas Morning News • *September 27, 1983*

Perot and his wife of nearly 36 years continue to reside in North Dallas.

"The question I've often been asked is, 'Why would Margot marry you?' I still don't know the answer."

The Dallas Morning News • *July 6, 1986*

❑

The Perots maintain vacation homes in Bermuda and on a lake up near the Oklahoma border. Lake Texoma serves as the home port of the ex-naval lieutenant's flotilla, which includes several ocean-racing Cigarette speedboats.

"I've got all sorts of boats. But if I could keep one I'd keep the windsurfer. It's the least expensive—

only cost about $800—but it's fun. We'll see something and get it. I got a Hovercraft for Christmas. My son looks around sometimes and shakes his head. He calls it Toys 'R' Us."

The Dallas Morning News • July 6, 1986

Perot seems otherwise a man of modest tastes (a dessert hound, his favorite is peach ice cream).

❑

"I drive an '84 Oldsmobile. It is so old that my daughter has threatened to put a bumper sticker on it that says, 'This IS my father's Oldsmobile.'

CNN's "Inside Business" • January 5, 1992

Since 1968, Perot has been in much demand as a speaker, and he is usually happy to accept the invitations. Shortly after Election Day '88, his topics began to subtly shift. Perhaps it was age, perhaps it was the gradual assimilation of the triumphs and defeats of the preceding two decades; but Perot now seemed to be taking a broader view of the world around him.

❑

"It's stock-taking time. The election is over and the nation wishes our next president the best of luck.

"We're at a critical time in our country's history. We are busy spending our children's money in enormous amounts. Unless we stop doing this soon, there is a very serious possibility that we will be the first generation of Americans that fails to leave a better life to our children.

"We are now the largest debtor nation in the history of man; 10 years ago we were the largest creditor nation. We're the most violent, crime-ridden nation in the industrialized world. We're also the biggest user of illegal drugs; we have five percent of the world's population, and we're using 50 percent of the the world's annual output of cocaine. Nine out of 10 of the largest banks in the world are now Japanese; the 10th is an American bank, but if you took the Third World loans out of it, it would be insolvent.

"Nowadays we treat our most serious domestic problems like a crazy aunt that we keep in the basement. Everybody knows she's there but nobody talks about her. But one day she's going to get loose and kill a neighbor."

The Washington Post • November 20, 1988

❑

"As I study Congress, they work hard; we don't pay them enough. Now I'd be really weird here.

I'd want to pay them enough, and then I would take all these lobbyist fees and throw them overboard. I'd take all those honorariums and say, I want you guys to belong to somebody—you bet—the American people.

"But they have to maintain two homes, they have to [go] back and forth. We don't pay them enough to do all that. Fix that—cost us nothing.

"We can't lose another year on scandals; we've got to go to work."

PBS's "American Interests" • September 16, 1989

❑

"We are like a person who is getting close to a heart attack.

"Let's stop thinking about re-election and start thinking about the American people and start putting in permanent fundamental changes."

CNN's "Inside Business" • January 5, 1992

❑

"All right, first thing you've got to do on business is get rid of all this crazy stuff we do on international trade. The way you get rid of that is to get rid of all these ex-government officials that cash in and become lobbyists for 300,000 bucks a year. We pass a simple law.

"Pass a law that if you were elected or appointed or worked in Washington you cannot be a lobbyist for a foreign government, foreign individual, for 10 years. You go to Washington to serve, not to get rich."

CNN's "Larry King Live" • February 20, 1992

In Perot's public statements, he was increasingly decrying an America he saw as weakened by an Everest of debt, by bloat in both industry and government and by misdirected foreign policies (discussed more fully in Chapter Three: "Slouching Toward 2001"). These were issues on which he had been speaking his mind, with remarkable consistency, down through the decades.

In hindsight, it appears that as the blush of Desert Storm faded and the nation's competitive fires proved resistant to rekindling, Perot was preparing to back yet another cause: his own entry, at the age of 62, into the epicenter of American politics.

❑

2

Crusader Or Quixote?

❑

"I will confirm that from time to time, I have responded to requests from the American government to help Americans in distress."

The Washington Post • *December 2, 1986*

❑

"I've been doing this for four presidents; there's nothing new about it.

"Someone said, 'Why didn't they call on you before 1969?' Hell, I didn't have any money before 1969."

Dallas Times Herald • *December 9, 1986*

Not long after the EDS public offering in 1968 had made him wealthy, according to Perot, he heard from the Nixon Administration on a matter more substantive than another campaign donation.

❑

"It was Henry Kissinger who got me involved with POWs, and my original contact was an Army colonel nobody ever heard of then, Alexander Haig."

Life • February 1988

❑

"[Kissinger] said, 'Look, [our] prisoners are dying from torture and neglect. We're going to Vietnamize the war, but it's going to take three years. Half the men are going to die. We want you to take your own money and embarrass the North Vietnamese into changing the treatment."

The Dallas Morning News • June 29, 1986

Ex-Annapolis grad Perot had been following the war closely because friends and acquaintances from his service days were fighting and dying in The Big Muddy.

In the period that the White House called, Perot was preparing to sponsor a national drive known as "United We Stand." Its goal was to build, by way of a media campaign soliciting calls and letters, bipartisan public support for an estimated 1,400 Americans held prisoner in North Vietnam.

Even as Perot followed through with that project, he began planning a more dramatic gambit. By late December, he had leased two Braniff International cargo jets, slapped giant red holiday ribbon decals on the fuselages, and loaded on board medical supplies, clothing, and 1,400 vacuum-sealed food packs. Inside each: ham, chicken, cranberry sauce, plum pudding, candied yams, nuts and candy—a complete Christmas meal.

Perot took off from Dallas with highly curious journalists in tow. After flying across the Pacific, he tried to meet with North Vietnamese representatives in a number of Southeast Asian nations in order to get permission to fly on to Hanoi. Finally, after Christmas had come and gone, it was suggested that he try mailing his 26 tons of relief goods to North Vietnam. The nearest post office acceptable to Hanoi? Moscow.

"It may be the largest postal bill in Russian history."

The Dallas Morning News • December 28, 1969

❑

"[In Moscow] we got through to [Soviet leaders] Brezhnev and Kosygin on the telephone. I think it was because nobody had ever tried to call them at home before."

New York Daily News • February 22, 1970

The Soviet Union refused, and returned the parcels to sender.

"The purpose of the Christmas trip was not to take packages to the prisoners, but to put the North Vietnamese in the position where they had to talk. We wanted to create a pressure-cooker situation where they had to see us. They didn't have to love us, but they had to see us."

The New York Times • February 28, 1971

Anecdotal evidence suggests that the lives of the POWs did in fact improve, even without the Christmas dinners.

Perot made several more trips to the war zone to press his mission. It was a crash course in media relations, for he learned to invite the press aboard his plane; on one trip, he even hosted a representative of that influential journal of political opinion, Women's Wear Daily.

He also learned that Communists could grasp capitalism under the right circumstances.

"First, we put [our sources] on a retainer. And the guys were getting paid for doing nothing. So we switched to the incentive program. We paid $100 for a picture that showed the head and shoulders of a prisoner. Another $100 for a shot that started from the toes and went up. And an additional $300 for pictures of those prisoners we hadn't heard about."

The Dallas Morning News • February 19, 1973

In March of 1972, Perot testified before a House subcommittee investigating the plight of POWs. He won permission to set up "tiger cages" inside the Capitol Building itself, at the center of the first floor. These were replicas of the cramped bamboo holding pens that the North Vietnamese used to incarcerate captured Americans.

❑

On accepting an award from the Disabled American Veterans for his POW mission:
"I'm honored and flattered you have chosen to present me with this plaque. I am also embarrassed because I think you've given it to me prematurely. There are still prisoners in North Vietnam.

"With your permission I'm going to put this away in one of my closets until these men are returned to their families, then I will display it proudly for the rest of my life."

The Dallas Morning News • February 24, 1970

❑

The next year, he underwrote a ticker-tape parade in San Francisco for a group of returning POWs despite pressure from Nixon aide H.R. (Bob) Haldeman to cancel it so as not to steal the thunder from a planned White House reception.

"That guy was your classic instance of someone who got to where he was because he was good at blowing up balloons in the campaign. He said if we went through with it there could be no military bands. Imagine! I told him, 'Fine, we'll get every high school band we can find. But when the subject of why we didn't have military bands comes up, I'll let them know about our little conversation.' Guess what? We got the military bands."

The Washington Post, April 12, 1987

❑

On the fallout from his POW campaigns:

"For three years I took a heck of a beating for trying to pull off a grandstand play. [At the time] I couldn't explain that the government had asked me to do it."

Life • *February 1988*

Long after the last American helicopter flew out of Saigon—from the roof of the U.S. Embassy in 1975, with those on board muscling off civilians poignantly seeking to cling to the landing struts—and long after the U.S. government declared that there were no captive Americans alive in Communist Southeast Asia, Perot continued his quest for a proper and decent ac-

counting of the nation's Missing In Actions.

He had been appointed during Ronald Reagan's first term to the President's Foreign Intelligence Advisory Board (PFIAB). In the mid-1980s, armed with top-level security clearance from the White House, Perot began burrowing through government archives for evidence that the MIA issue had been ignored for political reasons (discussed more fully, because of its implications for Campaign '92, in Chapter Six: "If You Build It, He Will Run").

In the late 1980s, he served once more as a go-between when Washington and Hanoi tried to finally put the POW/MIA issue to rest.

"The whole process is like making sausage. It may end up tasting good, but you don't really want to watch it being made."

Life • February 1988

❑

Perot still keeps in touch with a number of MIA families. And he still sponsors private investigations into alleged sightings of non-Asians being held in rain forests across the Pacific.

(In May of 1992, several Nixon aides suggested in public that Perot had been a sycophantish conniver whose Christmas flight to Hanoi was just another way to ingratiate himself with the White House. A check of many of the post-Watergate mea culpa memoirs

published by this inner circle reveals little if any mention of a short, jug-eared Texas billionaire.)

Off-the-shelf Missions

In 1979, ten months after Perot's private SWAT team emerged from Iran with two EDS executives who had been imprisoned in Tehran, the Ayatollah Khomeini's legions captured the U.S. Embassy and took 52 Americans hostage.

❑

On being asked by the Carter Administration for advice on possible rescue scenarios:

"By the end of December, we were so convinced that the method they had chosen wouldn't work, we felt the most responsible thing we could do would be to pull out—as a symbolic act.

"I remember one night they were sitting around the table [in Washington, D.C.] talking about how many Iranians we could afford to kill. When they came to me, I said, 'You can't let your mind go beyond protecting the 52 hostages and the Delta team. What are you going to tell our men—you can shoot the first 50? Why are we having this conversation?'"

D Magazine • January, 1984

Jimmy Carter's National Security Advisor, Zbigniew Brzezinski, took a dimmer view of Perot's can-do credo, as applied to foreign policy. In an April 12, 1987 interview with The Washington Post, he said, "There are all sorts of people who like to see themselves as actors on the great world stage. Armand Hammer, for example. They're often self-promoters. Usually they're not harmful or pains in the neck, so long as they don't do any damage. They're never shy. I'm always more impressed by people who are praised by others rather than praise themselves. I've seen [Perot] on TV. He's no wallflower, that's for sure."

Whether or not Perot ended up at the planning table through the government's invitation, or his own, the next series of global adventures that he bankrolled—literally—came at the behest of a Marine he'd first met in 1973. Oliver North had applied for a job at EDS; Perot, as a favor to North's commander, persuaded the young man to remain in uniform. By the beginning of the Reagan Administration, North was working on sensitive foreign policy issues as a National Security Council aide with an office in the basement of the White House.

In 1981, Perot was asked by North to covertly provide ransom money for U.S. Brigadier General James Dozier, kidnapped in Italy by a terrorist faction. He agreed, but Dozier was safely rescued before the money could be transferred.

Several years later, Perot was asked by North to ransom CIA Beirut station chief William Buckley, taken by a fundamentalist faction. The payment was never made, perhaps because the terrorists had already tortured Buckley to death.

❑

On trusting North's authority:
"I assumed that everything had been properly cleared because I've worked with the National Security Council for so many years. My sense has always been it's very well organized, very well controlled. I've never met a loose cannon in the National Security Council."

Dallas Times Herald, February 24, 1987

❑

On a D.C. dinner in late 1985, before what Ronald Reagan did or did not know came into question:
"The President thanked me for all I was trying to do to recover [CIA man] Buckley. It was absolutely clear what he was referring to—the payments were all I did for Buckley."

ABC's "This Week with David Brinkley" • December 7, 1986

❑

On explaining to North why he wouldn't covertly aid Nicaragua's contras:
"[It was one of the] lessons of Vietnam. You first commit the nation before you commit the troops."

The Washington Post, April 12, 1987

❑

"Now, the government's never approached me on that one, interestingly enough. Some of the private groups have come around to see me, and I said, 'Look, if we're going to have a war in this country, Congress has got to make that decision, not private individuals.'"

ABC's "This Week with David Brinkley" • December 7, 1986

❑

Ronald Reagan spent the final two years of his second term trying to rebottle the destructive genie of Iran-contra. Congress and a special prosecutor were soon probing the Ludlumesque skein of events, which had taken place on four continents and been orchestrated in part out of the White House basement.

Perot kept a low profile—until his covert contacts over the years with Ollie North began to surface. His opinions may have seemed a bit off-the-wall at the time, but not when viewed within the context of his

PFIAB service and his past access to the U.S. intelligence community.

"There are things going on in Washington around this whole Iran arms deal-contra thing. We should have been able to see that coming. If you are a real student you should have been able to see it coming, oh, back in the mid-Seventies—long before Reagan was even in the White House.

"It is the same team of beautiful people selling arms around the world. This is not a new experience for them to be selling arms at a profit. I mean some of them got caught once, in Australia. They got caught again in Hawaii. Edwin Wilson got put in jail. And if you go back and follow the trail, these guys have been working together since the Bay of Pigs. And yet now, suddenly, it is all coming into focus. And we will clean it up."

Barron's • February 23, 1987

❑

"When the dust settles on this thing and we can put it into perspective, I think we'll conclude that Admiral [John] Poindexter and Colonel [Oliver] North were bit players, and the major characters were people who were in the weapons business for years, some of whom had CIA connections.

"Those characters are all patriots in their own

minds. The True Path is in their heads. Their purpose in life is to save the country from the rest of us. Now, once a guy gets that in his head, get out of the way.

"If you went into covert activity and went into the field for years, well, you have no family life, no friends, the only people you had contact with were on the other side. You're an old man as a young man in that business. Talk about a recipe for instability—there it is. What do you do with these guys once you get them wound up and programmed? How do you shut them up in a free society? I guess in a totalitarian society you'd just put them away."

The Washington Post • April 12, 1987

Perot's charity toward Ollie North evaporated in late 1990 with the publication of "Under Fire." In his book, the ex-Marine states that shortly after Iran-contra broke, the Texan visited him and tried to persuade North to shield President Reagan, even offering monetary inducements.

❑

"I went to meet with Lieut. Col. North and his attorney, and I proposed the following. I told them in the meeting that I thought that a man who was prepared to die for his country should be prepared to tell the truth for his country, and that it looked terrible for a Naval Academy graduate to take the Fifth Amendment. And if they would simply tell the truth, put all the facts on the table and get this over with in a few days, I would pay his legal bills, take care of his family if he went to jail and help him get started when he got out."

ABC's "Good Morning America" • October 22, 1991

❑

"I am a former Naval Academy graduate myself—that's why this touched a nerve with me. You were trained in the Naval Academy to stand up like a man and tell the truth.

"I tried to talk to [North], but he won't talk to me. He won't return my calls. He's running and hiding like a scared rabbit.

"The thing that bothers me more than the inaccuracies is that a man who wouldn't tell the truth [before Congress], later wants to sell it [by way of 'Under Fire']. I think that's wrong."

The Dallas Morning News • October 23, 1991

❑

On the prospects for behind-the-scenes missions for the White House in the future:

"A guy calls you at three in the morning, you don't say, 'Well, have the president call me in the morning.' If you were in my situation and someone called you up at three in the morning and you could save a guy's life by writing a check that didn't mean anything to you, you'd do it, right? Sure you would. If someone said, 'Well, go outside and pick a flower and you can save someone's life,' you'd say sure. Now I say if these guys ever call me again for anything, I'm going to want a joint resolution from Congress, a note from the president and a legal opinion from the chief justice. Then I'll start to think about it."

The Washington Post • *April 12, 1987*

The Bong Show

"The number one criminal and social problem facing the state of Texas is narcotics. Narcotics officers live in a world only dimly perceived by the law abiding citizens of this state. They work 60-70 hours a week, associating with the worst elements of society. Their lives are frequently at risk. There is little public recognition of their work."

The Dallas Morning News • *December 15, 1979*

On narcotrafficking:
"It's the best business in Texas, if you have no scruples."

The Dallas Morning News • April 15, 1980

❑

On the Texas judiciary's passivity to the drug problem:
"Go out to a rural airport, park your car and watch what goes on in the middle of the night. [But] we've got judges in Texas who find no probable cause for search when a plane flies in with no lights on, landing on a dirt strip."

The Dallas Morning News • April 16, 1980

❑

"We want the guy at the top, you see. You first have to decide what you want to hunt—squirrels or bull elephants. We want bull elephants. If you get the man at the top, you break up the organization. If all you get is the guy at the bottom, you haven't done anything."

The Dallas Morning News • June 2, 1980

❑

"We ought to quit putting teen-agers in jail for stealing hubcaps if we can't put the big guys in jail for drug trafficking."

The Dallas Morning News, February 5, 1981

Perot had no record of law-and-order zealotry. But in bringing himself up to speed on the problem, he voiced his consternation at the lack of community support for police officers.

The issue was brought home when two Texas narks became involved in a sting that went sour in the city of Tyler. During the ensuing shoot-out, the male officer was seriously wounded. Perot learned that the pair might be in danger not only from traffickers, but perhaps also from corrupted elements of the law enforcement community. He promptly moved them to a safe house on one of his properties. (Some years later the uninjured female officer in that operation, Kim Ramsey Wozencraft, published the well-received novel "Rush," about a female undercover agent-turned-drug addict, which was adapted into a movie starring Jennifer Jason Leigh).

Not surprisingly, Perot developed some hard-nosed proposals to help the men and women in blue that outraged civil libertarians.

❑

On the need for sterner anti-drug laws:

"We have to to have a wiretap bill if we're going to get the people at the top."

The Dallas Morning News • April 16, 1980

❑

On computerizing police intelligence on a state-wide basis:

"A little piece of information from El Paso and a little piece from Texarkana and a little piece from Dallas is the way the drug dealers are finally stopped.

"This [computer system] will be very controlled by the state. The minute you talk about that, all the criminal lawyers jump up and say you are going to violate somebody's rights. Well, that's not true, I won't have access to the computer."

The Dallas Morning News • June 2, 1980

❑

The sterner laws enacted by the Texas legislature in 1981 did little to stem the problem of drug abuse. Perot, who consulted with Nancy Reagan before she launched her equally ill-fated "Just Say No" program, continued to rail against the evils of narcotics.

On the drug problem in Dallas:

"If you had one hour, I'd take you to southeast Dallas and show you Fort Apache. That's what it is, Fort Apache. The Jamaican drug dealers go around with firepower something like the Delta team would have. And we send police officers in there."

Dallas Times Herald • *March 13, 1988*

❑

"Just don't tinker with [narcotics]. It makes as much sense to drink Lysol. Now that's just plain Texas talk. Matter of fact, if you've got to do it, just drink Lysol and get it over with. O.K.? Save the taxpayers a lot of money."

Commencement address • *Austin College, 1989*

"Colombia only has [a drug] problem because we buy the cocaine. Fellas, let's get the Orkin man out here. And let's get rid of this stuff and you're not going to be able to do it softly or gently."

PBS's "American Interests" • *September 16, 1989*

But America's drug addiction continues to defy even draconian measures. To date, each new "war" launched against Colombian Marching Powder—even by a bulldog billionaire—has ended up the domestic equivalent of Vietnam.

❑

No Pass, No Play

On achieving millionairedom in 1968 and setting up the Perot Foundation to handle his philanthropy, the first sizable donation Perot made was to the school district encompassing the black ghettos of South Dallas. Its purpose: to fund a pilot program to help the disadvantaged children enter mainstream America. In the years that followed, education continued to be a major area of donations for Perot.

Thus, Texas Governor Mark White, a Democrat, was not merely offering to pad an influential businessman's resume when he offered Perot the chair of a panel to suggest reforms for the state's ailing public school system.

As Perot and the committee toured various school districts, he began to speak out thematically on the need for changes.

On the teacher's life:
"A really bad day in business is not as tough as a typical day in the public schools."

The Dallas Morning News • July 30, 1983

❑

"Japan, with no natural resources, a small land area and large population has become the most productive nation on earth. A school system stressing learning and academic achievement was imposed by the United States on Japan at the end of World War II. This education system is credited with much of Japan's current success."

The Dallas Morning News • September 11, 1983

❑

"Education has long lead times. If the Texas school system is completely restructured by September 1984, it will produce the first college graduate in the year 2000."

The Dallas Morning News • September 11, 1983

❑

"We need a classic liberal arts education that should include not only generous doses of math and science, but it should also be a balance of, and include, real English and real literature—not sandbox literature and English."

The Dallas Morning News • September 16, 1983

❑

"I'm trying to stir this pot so openly that whatever it is the people of Texas want will come to the surface."

The Dallas Morning News • September 18, 1983

"You may have read about the student who was out 15 days taking his chicken to agricultural contests.

"The first several times I inquired, I was told the [State Board of Education] had no authority [over extracurricular activities]. I finally sent a lawyer in, and under the code the state board has the authority to regulate these activities but never exercised that authority and instead for years was just fretting about it. Now that's the difference between leadership and status quo."

The Dallas Morning News • March 11, 1984

❑

On competency exams for teachers:
"If you're a fifth grade math teacher and you can't knock the top out of a fifth grade math test, you're in trouble as a fifth grade math teacher."

The Dallas Morning News • March 11, 1984

❑

"If I really thought the public did not want a better school system, I would do something else. I could be on a yacht somewhere."

The Dallas Morning News • March 26, 1984

❑

"The problem with our schools is that we are trying to do everything. We have to narrow our scope and focus on academics. We must use the traditional school day for learning. We must keep school nights free for homework."

The New York Times • April 2, 1984

❑

"There is no accountability in the public school system—except for coaches. You know what happens to a losing coach. You fire him. A losing teacher can go on losing for 30 years and then go to glory."

The Dallas Morning News • April 19, 1984

❑

On social, rather than academic, grade promotions: "It's the cruelest trick we play on minorities. We institutionalize economic segregation for life."

The Washington Post • May 31, 1984

❑

"There is no place for compromise. Better ideas, certainly—but not for compromise."

The Dallas Morning News • June 6, 1984

On criticism of his plans for school reform:

"What gets me are these guys who fret about having to make passing grades at a place like Highland Park High School. They don't have any idea of what life's like in some sections of South Dallas.

"When people who live on the hard side of town are mad at me over this, they get much more sympathy from me than the other side of town. I laugh at a lot of that stuff being said at Highland Park. Most of those guys have daddies who will be taking care of them whether they pass or not."

The Dallas Morning News • March 7, 1985

❑

"Texas, if it rides just on oil and gas, will become an Appalachia. With services, it can be a rich state. We look smart because God put so much wealth under the ground. But our children are going to grow up in a world of rapid change. The average person will change careers five times. For that he needs a fully developed intellect."

Fortune • July 8, 1985

Along the way, Perot began identifying the groups he held responsible for the problems. In high-school-football-crazy Texas, chief among these was the powerful scholastic sports establishment. His proposal—that students who are academically deficient lose their athletic eligibility—stirred twister-intense passions across the state and gave the entire reform package a catchy though over-simplified handle: No Pass, No Play.

❑

"I thought I was living pretty good until I found a school system that had towel warmers and towel coolers for the football team.

"[Texas school systems] do not exist for the benefit of the building contractors, the athletic-supply salesmen, the schoolbook publishers, not even for the benefit of Astroturf salesmen."

The Dallas Morning News • January 11, 1983

❑

"I asked [one district] superintendent, a former coach, about the balance between extra-curricular and academic activities. I asked, 'Is the tail wagging the dog?' He replied, 'Ross, there is no dog left, but that is what the people want.'

"For example, one school district gave a winning coach a salary greater than the superintendent. The superintendent and principal then received salary increases to correct this problem. At this point, the district had exceeded its budget and teachers' salaries were cut to resolve the problem.

"(If your reading skills allow you to finish this [3,000-word] article, please pause to reflect that many of our Texas high school graduates do not have the vocabulary, reading skills or concentration to read such material.)"

The Dallas Morning News • September 11, 1983

❑

On consolidating schools within a district:

"I'm for smaller schools. Large schools were created to produce winning football teams. They're a mistake. A child has no sense of individuality or sense of importance in a school that large."

The Dallas Morning News • September 16, 1983

❑

"The only difference [reform will make] is that the football team won't have a playbook that is as complicated as the Dallas Cowboys'. That some of the players won't be as developed because they wouldn't have such a junior-high farm system. The band might sound a few sour notes because it didn't have as much practice time. The drill team might have one curve in its line. But everybody will be there, and everybody still will have a good time."

The Dallas Morning News • October 1, 1983

❑

"We can still have football, but we can't continue to eat up our school days. High school football is a big source of entertainment in a lot of [Texas] towns. I intend on going into these towns and asking these people, 'Do you want adult entertainment, or do you want your kids to learn?'"

The New York Times • October 9, 1983

❑

"A losing coach is going to either get fired, or made a principal."

The Dallas Morning News • May 13, 1984

Nor were other traditional extracurricular activities exempt from Perot's criticisms.

❑

"We should eliminate high school programs whose real purpose is to allow students to leave school part-time to earn money to pay for cars.

"We should have vocational educational

courses that train students on modern equipment for jobs that exist."

The Dallas Morning News • September 11, 1983

❑

"[Our] children are going to have to grow up and go to work, and they don't know anything. They may have a heck of a time on Friday nights in high school, but for the rest of their life they're derelicts."

The Dallas Morning News • September 18, 1983

❑

"If you want to see raw terror on the face of a principal, let a cheerleader mama show up at school."

The Washington Post • May 31, 1984

Perot was more sympathetic to teachers, but only those he considered committed. Among his more controversial measures was a competency test (not unlike the one Governor Bill Clinton got enacted in Arkansas) that the teacher's union strongly opposed.

❑

On seniority-based raises for teachers:

"Nobody gets paid extra for staying alive."

The Dallas Morning News • August 25, 1983

"Teachers found to be marginal or unqualified should be removed from the profession. The schools of education that prepare future teachers are, with a few notable exceptions, doing a poor job.

"In one major school district, four out of five newly graduated teachers are found to be incompetent, and yet a Texas college of education has given them a certificate to teach. That's part of the reason why Texas ranks 44th in the quality of teachers coming out of its colleges of education.

"Correcting this problem carries the highest priority."

The Dallas Morning News • September 11, 1983

❑

On opposition from teachers colleges, which he strongly urged be reformed:

"The biggest argument from these folks is, 'You're going to put untrained teachers in the classroom.' I say, look, this is like a witch doctor criticizing a faith healer."

The Dallas Morning News • March 11, 1984

In addition to conceiving reforms, Perot had to lobby for their enactment by referendum. Characteristically, he spent most of his energies appealing directly to voters.

"Interestingly enough, we spend more money per student in the senior high level. All the evidence indicates we should surround the small child with whatever resources are necessary so he can 'learn to learn.'"

The Dallas Morning News • September 11, 1983

❑

"We are going to win or lose [the reform effort] in Grassroots, Texas, because if the people want it, they are going to get it."

The Dallas Morning News • January 6, 1984

❑

"I went to a Who's Who of Texas, and I said, 'Look. You don't have to care about blacks, you don't have to care about browns, you don't have to care about poor kids. But as long as you love money, you are going to have to care about what I'm talking about. A child's only chance in life is to get a good education.'

"And I said, 'Never forget: you could send him to Harvard for less than it costs to keep him in our state prison in Huntsville.' Now that's a fact."

ABC's "20/20" • April 3, 1986

❑

"Ranchers would sit there with their hats pulled down, squintin' and listenin'. I'd tell them it costs more to keep a man in the penitentiary than it does to send him to Harvard. One old guy stands up, pushes his hat back and says, 'Hell, Ross, the answer's simple. Send those jailbirds to Harvard.'"

Life • February 1988

❑

On the eve of the special legislative session to consider academic reforms:

"When you get right up to reform, some folks get real rabbity."

The Washington Post • May 31, 1984

Some of the reforms proposed by Perot's committee were voted into existence, including "No Pass, No Play," teachers' raises and preschool programs. Others were turned down, including the measure mandating competency tests for public school teachers. In fact, the education lobby lent its weight to the successful effort to unseat Mark White when the governor sought a second term in 1986.

In the years since, Perot has maintained an active interest in education in America. And he has attempted to deliver his sermon in language to appeal to a diverse cross-section of the nation's adults.

❑

"We have a history in Texas of saying, 'Oh, he's a good hand.' That means he's a good hand. But in the new Texas we need to be able to say, 'He's got a good head.' We've got more than enough people to string barbwire fence, to do manual labor. And we've got a steady stream coming out of Mexico. We need people with fully developed intellects to support our state's future."

ABC's "Business World" • November 6, 1988

❑

"Seventy-five percent of our young people think that the president during the Vietnam War was Franklin Roosevelt."

"ABC's "Business World" • January 31, 1988

❑

"In a recent worldwide algebra test we ranked 14th out of 15 nations tested. If it makes you feel any better, we beat Thailand."

The Washington Post • November 20, 1988

❑

"Seventy-five percent of high school seniors don't know who Whitman or Thoreau is. Twenty-five percent of college seniors in Texas can't name the country on Texas' southern border. That's scary."

Texas Monthly • *December, 1988*

❑

"Almost as hard as facing up to the fact that while Texas has a large and diverse population, our school system was essentially built on the assumption that the only people considered educable in our state were middle-income children whose mothers didn't work. In fact, we found that only one out of five children in the school system had mom sitting there at home to do the tutoring that the schools weren't doing. We were writing off the rest of our young people.

"One thing we decided didn't belong in the Texas schools is the policy of 'social promotion.' [Today], in our schools, you either earn promotion to the next grade or you don't get promoted. Interestingly enough, the minority parents in our state strongly support that. They now realize that social promotion is nothing but a cruel trick played on the young people, who end up economically segregated by their lack of skills and education.

"Being a melting pot for diverse cultures and heritages has always been one of America's greatest strengths. We don't have time to waste fighting one another on the race issue. We should love one another. If we can't do that we should learn to get along with one another now. The few die-hards remaining should recognize that we are stuck with one another."

The Washington Post • November 20, 1988

❑

"We have the least literate work force in the industrialized world. Reading to children one hour on television is good free campaign advertising for the next campaign."

CNN's "Inside Business" • January 5, 1992

❑

3

Slouching Toward 2001

❑

"Now the average citizen can't relate to a billion or a trillion. A million dollars in thousand-dollar bills is a stack of thousand-dollar bills, four inches high. A billion dollars in thousand-dollar bills is 300 feet high. A trillion dollars in thousand-dollar bills extends from the top of [this] table to 63 miles out in space."

CNN's "Inside Business, Pt.1" • January 5, 1992

If Perot's arithmetic is correct, his personal fortune, stacked in those bills that bear the portrait of Salmon P. Chase, would be taller than all but three of Manhattan's skyscrapers. In fact, it is most likely under a billion less than the entire U.S. budget for 1930, the year he was born.

Perhaps because he has so much money, he has brooded more than the average citizen over America's rapidly escalating national debt—and its consequences, which in Perot's opinion extend far beyond the push-me-pull-you of tax hikes and services cuts.

In the wake of the 1987 Wall Street crash:

"• The United States now has a $2.3 trillion debt

and will have a $3 trillion debt by 1989.

"• Our country, effectively, does not have a national budget. We avoid facing the budget issue by passing continuing resolutions that put us deeper into debt each year.

"• There is no correlation between taxes paid by the people and money spent by the government.

"Even if wealth and corporate profits were taxed at 100 percent, we could not begin to raise the money needed to operate our country. The taxes from millions of working Americans are essential to fund our country's needs. Obviously, if millions of our people are not working, not only will we be unable to pay our bills as a nation and individually, but we will have to somehow create huge make-work or welfare programs, at a time when the United States does not have the money."

The Washington Post • *October 25, 1987*

❑

"The crash was like a giant tapping us on the shoulder. But what have we done about the deficit? Nothing. What have we done about Third World loans? Nothing. What have we done about our savings and loan system? Nothing. We had this big shock. Everybody was frightened. But now we're just kind of bumbling along."

Wall Street Journal • December 30, 1987

❑

"The '80s is the decade that we gave away our industrial lead and acted totally irresponsibly in wrecking some of our big corporations through leveraged buyouts. We felt affluent because we were living off borrowed money. We've got to clean up the deficit, clean up the drugs, clean up the justice system, clean up industry. But right now it's like Lawrence Welk music: It's just wonderful, wonderful, wonderful. And nobody will fix it before it breaks."

Time • January 1, 1990

❑

"Say let's try to pay one year's debt.

"OK, we'll take all of the profits of the Fortune 500 companies—I wouldn't have half of what I needed.

"Let's get aggressive, let's confiscate the wealth of the Forbes 400—I wouldn't have enough money to pay this year's debt."

CNN's "Inside Business, Pt. 1" • January 5, 1992

"If the Germans, Japanese and Arabs... lose confidence in our country, and we can't sell short-term debt, not only does the music stop, the party's over and the ballroom got burnt."

CNN's "Inside Business, Pt. 2" • January 5, 1992

Running on Empty?

Tracking Perot's pronouncements over two decades, it becomes clear that he feels Americans themselves have been losing confidence in their country's private sector—and perhaps themselves.

To sum up his thesis: If the U.S. could again manufacture products good enough to compete in the international marketplace, it would cure the negative balance-of-payment crisis behind America's recent record deficits.

Perot had a first-hand look at the problem during his two years at General Motors, and he was pretty much a Johnny-one-note in blaming the majority of that corporation's woes on the occupants of its executive suites.

"At the end of World War II, we were the supplier to the world. Many of us who grew up in this era complain that the playing field is not level. But, in fact, the playing field is never level. Too many of us grew up in a world where Americans owned the bat, the ball, the stadium, both teams and the lights. That's all changed.

"We've got some first-class teams on the field—Germany had nowhere to go but up; Japan had absolutely no other way to go—and they're tearing our heads off. In 1951 Toyota was bankrupt. Today it is the No. 3 automaker in the world. The automobile capital of the world is no longer Detroit. It is Tokyo."

Dallas Times Herald • March 8, 1987

❑

In Perot's view, the lack of leadership that he believes pervades American corporations has a downward ripple effect.

"Apathy is a product of advanced technology. Since Sputnik, we have jammed kids full of facts but failed to develop them as people. Leadership is left to chance. The only place it is taught is in the armed forces. Even Harvard Business School doesn't teach it."

New York Daily News • February 22, 1970

❑

"There's not enough old-fashioned salesmanship today. I keep waiting for someone to sell me a new car. I take the car into the dealer for a checkup and they give me a checkup. They sit me down in an air-conditioned waiting room. They give me a magazine and a cup of coffee. But they don't try to sell me a new car."

The Dallas Morning News • June 19, 1971

Next day response: An ambitious salesman at a Dallas automobile dealership, unable to reach Perot by phone, drove a brand new luxury vehicle to the businessman's home—and was promptly escorted off the property.

❑

"Life's hard. It's always been and always will be. And life is tough in the air-conditioned house. People expect life to be easy."

The Dallas Morning News • October 12, 1972

❑

"Today, a factory in Taiwan paying their people pennies an hour compared to dollars an hour here, will still turn out more high quality finished units than American plants. That's a double-edged sword. Their quality is greater, their productivity is greater, but their pay is a fraction of ours."

Los Angeles Times • August 13, 1980

❑

"We now expect life to be so extraordinarily good to us that we must be paid $20 an hour for a job that you could train a monkey to do—or we think the world is being unfair."

The Saturday Evening Post • April, 1983

❑

"We must learn to compete and win in international competition. At this point, we are losing. We have watched steel, television, parts of the electronics industry, automobiles and other industries decline or disappear to international competition. Hundred of thousands of jobs formerly held by U.S. workers have been lost overseas. If we had kept our position in these industries, we would not be incurring the huge deficits we now have at the national level. The tax base from these jobs would have been more than adequate to cover these deficits."

The Dallas Morning News • September 11, 1983

❑

On more vocational training in public schools:
"The worst mistake we could make is to turn out large numbers of technological robots. The memory of the race, the rights of the next generation cannot be taught through advanced technology."

U.S. News & World Report • February 3, 1986

❑

"Let's just hunker down and beat [the Japanese] on blocking and tackling. That is how they beat us. Our solution is to go out and buy new uniforms. The team looks good, but it still can't play."

Wall Street Journal • July 22, 1986

❑

"If we did not have such a thing as an airplane today, we would probably create something the size of NASA to make one. It's a good thing the Wright Brothers didn't know any better when they made the machine fly."

Speech in Dallas to the Fall Joint Computer Conference • November, 1986

❑

"I can't think of one reason in the world why we can't paint a car better than the Japanese. As a matter of fact, I would hope that if you go down into [GM's] paint shop and say, 'Why the hell can't you guys paint a car better than the Japanese?' you'd get a good fight started. Now that would be real progress, in my mind."

Ward's Auto World • *November, 1986*

❑

On international trade competition:
"The greatest danger we have is the 'maybe it'll go away' syndrome. It ain't going away, it's going to get worse."

Dallas Times Herald • *December 9, 1986*

❑

"[At EDS] I've had guys come in and say, 'I've just got to be a vice president.' And I say, 'Fine, you are.' 'Give me a purple robe.' 'No, a purple robe costs a little money.' Titles cost nothing. Titles mean nothing. That's one of the problems in our country. We assign too much emphasis to titles and not enough emphasis to what you are doing."

Newsweek • *December 15, 1986*

❑

"One of the most startling things I have heard in recent months—and I am glad he said it—[then House Majority Leader] Jim Wright in his speech said that the principal export from New York harbor was scrap iron and waste paper going to Japan. That they are going to send us back from that scrap iron and waste paper, finished automobiles and electronic devices in cardboard boxes. Now this is not the America that we think we know; this is some kind of banana republic shipping out raw material."

Barron's • February 23, 1987

❑

"If you ever want to get anything done in a foreign country, you'd better understand their culture."

Dallas Times Herald • February 24, 1987

❑

"It used to be that if your parents gave you an orange for Christmas, you knew they still loved you. But if they gave you a Japanese toy, you wondered. Now [the Japanese] make the best stuff in the world. Just take a look around your house."

The Washington Post • April 12, 1987

"We have unfairly blamed the American worker for the poor quality of our products. The unsatisfactory quality and appearance of many of our products is the result of poor design and engineering—not poor assembly.

"You can literally see the difference between a car made in Japan and a car made in the United States by an American manufacturer. If you take a car made in Japan by Japanese workers and place it alongside a Japanese car made in a U.S. plant by U.S. workers (led by Japanese executives) there is no difference in quality. The Honda cars made in this country by U.S. workers are of such high quality that Honda intends to export them.

"Obviously, the American worker is not the problem. The problem is a failure of leadership."

The Washington Post • October 25, 1987

❑

"There's a book, 'Beyond Human Scale,' that every American should read. Maybe the dinosaur, for the average fellow like me, is the best example. He got so big he couldn't function. Big is not beautiful. We in America like to think big is beautiful. Big is inefficient.

"If you want to make something happen that's

cutting edge, best in the world, you get a small, high talent team, you go off and you don't come back until it's done."

ABC's "Business World" • November 6, 1988

The book Perot cited, by Eli Ginzberg and George Vojta, argues that the very largeness of modern corporations results in wasteful mismanagement. It echoes J.F. Schumacher's 1973 "Small Is Beautiful: Economics as if People Mattered," an underground best-seller embraced by—ironically—the then-governor of California, Jerry Brown.

❑

"Some people say that the loss of manufacturing leadership is no problem because our leading-edge high technology will bail us out. Not likely.

"In 1974, we developed 70 percent of the world's advanced technology. By 1984, our share was down to 50 percent. By 1994, it will be down to 30 percent. The Japanese are filing more patents each year in our own patent office than we are."

The Washington Post • November 20, 1988

❑

"The one thing I know through experience—the one absolute thing I know—is that people don't know why they come to work until they don't have to come to work. There's a very large number of people who are eagles, who do brilliant work, but who just fold up on you once their financial needs are met. They lose their edge. And it's a tightrope, because you have an obligation to reward those people for excellence, but some of them are going to go soft as a result. So you just have to keep training the new young ones behind them."

Inc. • *January, 1989*

❑

"A red ribbon isn't worth anything once you graduate. If your background is in music and you went to the Texas State Band Contest, you know they gave a five-foot statue for the band with the best personality. Everybody got a prize. That's not the way the real world is."

Commencement address, Austin College • *1989*

❑

"If you can't beat the Germans or the Japanese and you can still sleep soundly at night, you're not right for the job."

Fortune • July 3, 1989

❑

"Nineteen fifty-one, Toyota was bankrupt. Today, Toyota is the No. 3 carmaker in the world with $12 billion cash. Nineteen forty-six, Mr. Honda, a high school graduate, was walking around picking up pieces of scrap trying to make motor scooters. He is the No. 4 car manufacturer in the United States today."

PBS's "American Interests" • September 16, 1989

❑

"When I go to Asia or Europe, I feel like I'm looking at tomorrow. When I go to many U.S. cities, I see decay and neglect and I feel like I'm looking at yesterday."

Fortune • March 26, 1990

❑

"Certainly, we can be the leaders in the game again. But we can't do it if we just sit around and whine.

"There's an intelligent relationship between Japan and the businesses in Japan. There's an adversarial relationship in our country between government and business. The best and the brightest students coming out of Tokyo University—their top school—go to work for MITI, the Ministry of Trade, that controls all of this and makes the policy at a fraction of what they could make in industry to serve their country.

"Our best and brightest—yeah, our best and brightest go to Wall Street and become junk bond dealers. And the saddest case I ever heard of was a man with a Ph.D. from MIT that got his best offer doing program trading on Wall Street."

"CBS This Morning" • May 7, 1991

❑

"Japan is our rival, not our enemy. Japan is a competitor. The saddest thing that can happen to our country as we lose our competitive position is to start hating our competitors. That leads to great stress and leads to very unproductive thinking. Bashing a Toyota won't make a better car."

CNN's "Larry King Live" • February 20, 1992

Although Perot sometimes sounds like the Fifth Horseman of the Apocalypse, he can also display a wry wit about America's remaining assets.

❑

On surveying Miss USA 1985, Christine Fichtner, who had just hugged Perot on the dais of a celebratory dinner and called him "such a hunk of man":

"I don't think we have to worry about the Japanese producing one of these."

The Washington Post • April 12, 1987

Gordon Gekko Lives

In mid-May of 1992, Forbes magazine reported on its new survey of America's 800 largest publicly held companies. Nineteen ninety-one was marked by an ongoing recession, sagging corporate profits and widespread layoffs. Still, 407 of those 800 companies tendered its chief executive officer in excess of $1 million in total compensation. The number for 1990: 386. Perot seems to view such largesse as a character issue. And since his costly failed bail-out venture on Wall Street in the early 1970s, he has never hidden his distrust of corporate brass and financiers. Those suspicions were heightened during a series of high-stake negotiations in the spring of 1986.

"When we were selling EDS to General Motors, I noticed that we had the people down from New York and, once they got here, every time we had a good meeting, the stock would go up, and every time we had a bad meeting, it would go down.

"One day, I had one of my guys follow the people from my meeting at EDS to their hotel, and call me over the walkie-talkie radio when they got to the hotel. One minute later, the stock started to move. I called them back over here and said, 'Okay guys,' and I took them through it step by step. I said that was the end of that, because I am not going to put up with that. This is rocky stuff. And that was the end of that."

Barron's • February 23, 1987

Perot has consistently refused to name the New York lawyers and financiers who visited him in Dallas, but the names of the firms involved appear in SEC documents pertaining to the deal.

❑

"I, of course, know nearly everybody that runs the big companies in this country. A lot of them do fit into a pretty standard mold. Many of them fit into a mold to be personally unattractive to me. Certainly the people that I call the corporate gypsies, I have no use for at all, because they float from company to company, taking and not giving much... Their vision of the future is 90 days."

The Washington Post • July 7, 1985

"In Pontiac [Mich.], GM executive parking garages are heated while the poor guys who work in the plant freeze their tails off walking to work through the snow. It costs $140,000 a year to heat one parking garage. I'd shut that thing down; it has nothing to do with making cars."

Wall Street Journal • *November 25, 1986*

❑

On white-collar crime:

"I make no distinction between the MBA white-collar criminal and the kid who is a high school dropout who robs a 7-Eleven store, in terms of basic character.

"You can't expect the average people to support our system of justice unless it is fair. And you are dead right: The guy who commits conventional—what we perceive as conventional—minor theft, who comes from a lower income status, will do time. The guy who does a multimillion rip-off of some institution, or other investors, will probably wiggle his way out of it.

"I personally don't buy the theory that the ego hit and the character deterioration hit and all that a white-collar person takes is comparable to a jail sentence. You know the New York street saying:

BARBARA LAING - BLACK STAR

Ex-Navy man Perot keeps a fleet on Lake Texoma.

Perot lived his first 19 years in this three-bedroom.

SIPA

Grown up Ross is no 4-H Club fan.

SIPA

Perot's bent nose dates to his horse-taming days.

Perot spent two years at Texarkana Junior College (left and below) before entering the U.S. Naval Academy (right, on graduation day with bride-to-be Margot and his parents).

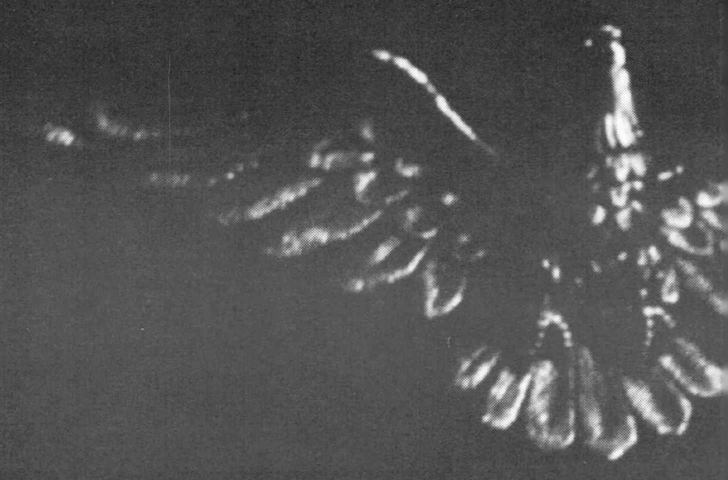

Six years after hatching the company, EDS's highest flier had a $200 million nest-egg.

SHEL HERSHORN

OCK
AT A TIME

In 1970, Perot toured North Vietnamese POWs being held in the South. He hoped Hanoi would reciprocate by letting him see American prisoners held in the North.

J.P. LAFFONT - SYGMA

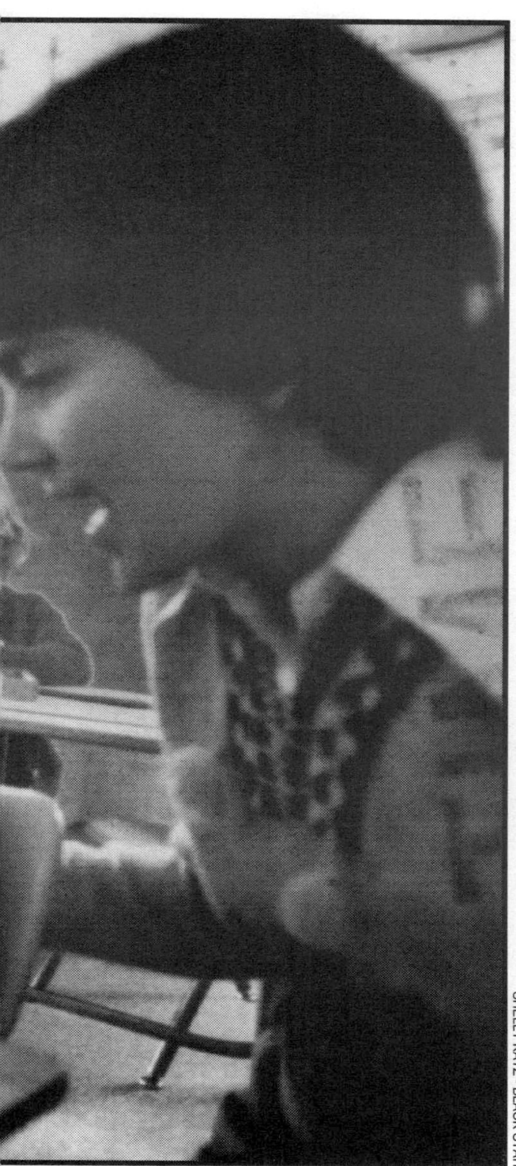

SHELLY KATZ - BLACK STAR

Perot's 1985 visit to a Dallas class came during his campaign to reform Texas schools. (His first sizable charitable donation had gone to an inner-city school in the late 1960s.)

AP / WIDE WORLD PHOTOS

Perot and GM's Roger Smith, a week after the divorce.

DAVID WOO - DALLAS MORNING NEWS

Prince Charles and Perot: Dallas was all ears.

ꓤON TOM - NBC / GLOBE PHOTOS

Richard Crenna played Perot in "On Wings of Eagles."

AKHTAR HUSSEIN - SIPA

Big things seem to happen to Perot on his birthdays.

AVID WOO - DALLAS MORNING NEWS

Margot and Ross wed in 1956 in Greensburg, Penn.

VID WOO - DALLAS MORNING NEWS

A rare public flocking of the Perot family in 1986.

AP / WIDE WORLD PHOTOS

Asked when he would announce his candidacy, Perot said, "Watch my lips."

'If you can't do the time, don't commit the crime.' It is pretty simple."

Barron's • February 23, 1987

❑

"We've got this funny phenomenon going that says, 'Why don't we get rid of all of our basic industries and go to a service economy?' The best and brightest out of Asia are learning basic industrial engineering skills that will create real jobs. Our best and brightest all go to Wall Street to play with paper, sell junk bonds or do leveraged buyouts. The priorities of the Asians are certainly much better than ours. We cannot give up our basic industries. This is a joke. Who are all these consultants, lawyers and accountants going to sell their services to? They can't sell to one another. This is the goofiest idea in the world. The service economy is a mirage."

Dallas Times Herald • March 8, 1987

❑

On the October, 1987 stock-market crash:

"A year ago, I couldn't make anything in the market make sense. There was too much money chasing too few stocks. Meanwhile, all the fundamentals on the instrument panel were in the red. So I pulled out a year early because I couldn't understand it.

"When you find a place like Wall Street where you're paying 28-year-old boys a half-million a year, you know something is off track. It has nothing to do with reality."

The New York Times • October 21, 1987

❑

"We Americans have evolved from a tough, resilient people, willing to sacrifice for future generations, into a people who want to feel good now—at any price—and let the future take care of itself. Put more directly, we have become credit junkies, shooting up huge sums of borrowed money on a government and personal level—looking for another high."

The Washington Post • October 25, 1987

❑

"When the history of junk bonds is written, I think the first sentence should be, 'Junk bonds, by definition, were junk.'"

ABC's "Business World" • November 6, 1988

❑

On Texas' savings and loan scandal:
"When we deregulated, the crooks showed up and realized: 'There it is, the bank.'

"Boy, there was a lot of pillaging and plunder. I'd put a lot of those guys in jail. If you can't do the time, don't commit the crime."

Dallas Times Herald • November 18, 1988

❑

"Somewhere off the coast of Vietnam floating in a boat is a young person who will probably drown or not ever reach freedom who is smarter than anyone here. Somewhere on the streets of India is a young person starving, smarter than anyone here. Working third shift in some factory in this country is a person smarter than anyone here... Take it from me, if you go through life with a generous dose of humility and feeling lucky rather than feeling special, you'll beat those cocky guys and girls ten times out of ten."

Commencement address, Austin College • 1989

❑

"If I set the curriculum at the Harvard Business School, God forbid, the first and most important course would be human nature."

Inc. • January, 1989

"Let's get right to it: The rules for success in these big corporations are not the rules of the marketplace. You don't get to be chairman of the board by building the best car, the best television set or the best stereo. You get to be chairman of the board by being good at running overhead projectors and making staff reports and not knowing what's going on on the factory floor. And only the dummies with dirt under their fingernails are in engineering."

PBS's "American Interests" • September 16, 1989

❑

"There's only two places in the world a 28-year-old can make half a million a year. That's selling dope and dealing in junk bonds. They're both destroying our country."

PBS' "American Interests" • September 16, 1989

❑

"In the Eighties, top management focused on golden parachutes, poison pills, financial tricks, and leveraged buyouts—things that had nothing to do with getting competitive. We have really trashed our big companies. In the Nineties we will pay for the excesses of the Eighties. Not only that, we'll have to do it when we're hopelessly leveraged— like a punch-drunk fighter."

Fortune • *March 26, 1990*

❑

On junk bonds:

"In one transaction [RJR Nabisco], the fees were over $1 billion. The average citizen asks, don't they have to give [the money] back if the company fails? No, it's paid. In this particular case, they have to earn $10 million a day in pretax earnings just to make the interest payments. In its history, that company has never come close to those kinds of pretax earnings on a daily basis. Now they'll have to restructure. That means laying people off. Or they can always raise the cost of food [RJR's major product area].

"If we're going to raise the price of food, who should get the money? The farmer, obviously. Not the bankers and the people who did these obscene deals that make no sense at all."

Management Review • *June, 1990*

❑

On the sentencing of junk-bond king Michael Milken, who drew time in federal prison, but was allowed to

keep a substantial proportion of his assets:
"What an obscene message. If a young person in Texas had just stolen four hubcaps, I guarantee you they wouldn't let him keep two.

"If you ever find a Michael Milken or a Donald Trump in your organization, have a public firing."

National Underwriter • *November 5, 1990*

❑

"I watch these CEO's wandering around with their blow-dried hair, their $3,000 suits, their 23-year-old trophy wives and I think, 'These are the stewards of millions of jobs.'"

The New York Times • *November 5, 1991*

❑

On CEO remuneration:
"I've said to these guys: 'If you want to make that kind of money, be a rock star. Go to baseball. You know, play baseball.' But if you want to run a company, you cannot have that kind of gap between the people who do the work and the people who run the company."

CBS's "60 Minutes" • *March 29, 1992*

❑

4

Wit And Wisdom

❑

"I am sort of like the fellow standing down by the side of the road in overalls. A Cadillac pulled up alongside of him and the driver asked him if he knew where New Boston was. The fellow answered no. Then the driver asked him if he knew where Gladewater was, and he said he didn't know where that was either. Finally this fellow in the Cadillac said, 'What in the world do you know?' The old fellow answered, 'I know I am not lost.'"

Testimony before the House Committee on Ways and Means • March 21, 1973

One trait of a master raconteur is the ability to deflect listeners from certain subjects with disarming grace. Despite his finely tailored suits, Perot likes to come across as a cracker-barrel sage from East Texas, setting on the porch of the general store, just tugging on a Dr. Pepper. It is a persona both seamless in its execution and effective in its cloaking powers.

Some of this undoubtedly stems from security precautions. Most folks in Dallas seem to know exact-

ly where the Perots live, but since 1968, at least, the family has tightly guarded its privacy. "Old Ross" often mentions his son, "Big Ross," with whom he's involved in business projects like Alliance Airport, and his four daughters, but reveals little about them. Even good, meaty profiles of Perot offer little insight into his tastes beyond a passion for Americana, a marina's worth of pleasure boats and barbeque sandwiches followed by peach ice cream.

But the man who can buy anything (and, most likely, anyone) more than compensates for his reticence about personal matters with a willingness to share his distilled knowledge on those subjects most people probably want to hear about, anyway: money and his keys to success.

It's Easy for Him to Say

"Making all this money is partly an accident. I could have put the same amount of energy into a corporation that made steel forgings, but I would have been in the wrong place at the wrong time."

Fortune • November, 1968

Perot holds almost mythically traditional views about the value of a dollar, as well the responsibilities of those privileged to have more than enough. His is a financial credo that seems to have stayed remarkably con-

sistent over more than two decades.

"I pay taxes on all the money before it goes into the [Perot Foundation]. I think the federal government is a charitable cause, too."

Los Angeles Times • November 27, 1969

❑

On whether his Christmas, 1969, flight to Hanoi qualified as an IRS write-off:
"I can think of lots of better ways to cut down on taxes than by flying 35,000 miles in 12 days."

The Dallas Morning News • January 11, 1970

❑

"I don't plan to leave my money to my children. I think the greatest legacy I can leave my children is this great country and the great opportunity I have had."

Testimony before the House Committee on Ways and Means • March 21, 1973

❑

"I expect to be taxed generously in the future as

I have in the past.

"While some have come before you talking about sheltered Americans who pay no taxes, I do not fit into that category."

Testimony before the House Committee on Ways and Means • March 21, 1973

On a Reagan proposal for higher gasoline taxes:
"Bad highways and bridges are a drain on our economy, and it is vital that they are rebuilt. The gasoline tax is an indirect form of a toll road. The road user pays through this tax. I don't have a better idea for raising the money needed for this vital work, so until one comes along, I will have to go along with it. There's not enough money in general revenue to pay for the rebuilding."

The Saturday Evening Post • April, 1983

❑

"Wealth moves into different hands. Neither Sam Walton [the late founder and chairman of Wal-Mart] nor I, who apparently are America's two wealthiest men, had much money at all 20 years ago."

Fortune • September 1, 1986

❑

"I can't think of anything worse than a person in my position to be grasping for some tax advantage. I'm delighted to pay big taxes. Big taxes means big income."

The New York Times • April 15, 1988

❑

"People have been trying to get me to buy sports teams for years. I always ask, 'How much does it cost, and how much does it make?' The place gets really quiet in a hurry."

Texas Monthly • December, 1988

❑

"Money is the most overrated thing in the world. Tangible things don't bring happiness; happiness is a state of mind. I've lived across the economic spectrum... I grew up in the Depression and assumed 'hard' was normal. When I was 6, I went to the 1936 opening of the state fair. I remember the cars on display. It never occurred to me then that I'd ever own a car, let alone be the largest shareholder in General Motors. That's the kind of world we live in."

USA Weekend • February 17, 1989

❑

To students of the Harvard Business School:
"Guys, just remember, if you get real lucky, if you make a lot of money, if you go out and buy a lot of stuff—it's gonna break. You got your biggest, fanciest mansion in the world. It has air conditioning. It's got a pool. Just think of all the pumps that are going to go out. Or go to a yacht basin any place in the world. Nobody is smiling, and I'll tell you why: Something broke that morning. The generator's out; the microwave oven doesn't work; the captain's gay; the cook's quit. 'Things' just don't mean happiness."

Fortune, September 11, 1989

❑

"One day, a reporter from Australia was in my office when [son] Ross walked in. 'So, young man,' says the reporter, 'how does it feel to be the son of the richest man in Texas?' Ross just stared at him. 'Mister,' he said, 'all I know is I get 25 cents a week.'

"It's important to give your kids a lot of rope—sons especially."

Fortune, September 10, 1990

❑

On backing Oklahoma Senator David Boren's 1990 bill to hike long-term capital gains and income taxes on affluent Americans:

"I think [Boren] was somewhat intrigued that I was saying I should be taxed more. I don't think he was being run over in the halls up there by people saying the same thing."

Wall Street Journal, October 18, 1990

❑

"I think everybody in this country that's doing honest, hard work outdoors—farming all day, laying pipelines, doing whatever they're doing—would be delighted to swap places with a fellow sitting in the office making money with money. Money doesn't take a vacation. Money doesn't get a day off on Christmas or Easter or Thanksgiving. Money works 24 hours a day, seven days a week. I can't think of one reason why I should pay less [taxes] than people doing honest work."

CBS's "America Tonight" • October 24, 1990

Action Is Character

"I'm used to being able to say something once, in a whisper, and have committed guys around this country to go make it happen."

The New York Times • March 25, 1973

Perot's exhortations about the need to take decisive action and to assume personal responsibility have an almost pulp-fiction aura about them—yet rarely ring false. Perhaps it is the challenges he has taken on; perhaps it is the palpable confidence of his delivery; perhaps it is the Knute Rockne-ish powers of persuasion that, three decades ago, enabled him to meet one year's sales quota in 19 days.

"In anything you get ready to do, there are always people that tell you you can't do it, or give you, you know, a lot of reasons why you shouldn't give it a good try and my style has always been to sort of brush those things aside and get face to face with the issue and see what real problems materialize."

ABC's "Issues and Answers" • January 11, 1970

❑

"There are people who climb into the ring and there are people who sit in the stands. Those who sit in the stands always seem to know more about the game than those in the ring."

The Dallas Morning News • January 11, 1970

❑

"I don't mind the people that feel strongly one way or the other about the [Vietnam] war. It's the people that don't feel at all that get me."

New York Daily News • February 22, 1970

❑

"I'm extremely successful in attracting people who are better people than I am. And then I leave them alone to succeed or fail. There's no motivation like leaving a man alone to do the job."

New York Daily News • March 14, 1970

❑

"If something needs to be done, pull together a small team, and give them a defined task and the resources to get it done."

Look • March 24, 1970

❑

"Everyone has his role. Some are in the arena, others are in the grandstand. It's the ones in the arena who get bloody noses and get skinned up.

"The greatest thing that happens to me is the skeptics. Unless someone says 'He's never going to get it done,' I'm not sure I'd get it done, really.

"But the people in the grandstand serve a useful purpose, they drive the ones in the arena on. That's gas in the car, as far as I'm concerned.

"The only thing I'd change is the fact that skeptics always seem to leave five minutes before the end of the game. You just want to be able to wink and say, 'How about that?'"

Women's Wear Daily • *April 13, 1970*

❑

"We live in a time when it's in vogue to point out the problems of the world. It's in vogue to hold seminars and develop theoretical knowledge on how to solve the problem of hunger, but it would be poor form to go out and feed somebody.

"We say 'We are the elite; let's define the problems and lesser men will come along and solve them!' There is a very delicate balance between people who produce more than they use and those who can't produce what they need. Every social problem we have should try to bring those who can't produce up to a break-even point, to make taxpayers out of them."

The Dallas Morning News • *October 12, 1972*

❑

"Any company that spends a lot of time on internal fighting will lose the battle against the competition. It's always going to be beaten by a company that operates as a team."

Wall Street Journal • *July 22, 1986*

❑

"The first EDSer to see a snake kills it. At GM, the first thing you do is organize a committee on snakes. Then you bring in a consultant who knows a lot about snakes. Third thing you do is talk about it for a year."

Business Week • *October 6, 1986*

❑

"Well, there was no law when Teddy Roosevelt stepped out [on] center stage. He was a good Republican. He was supposed to represent, I guess at that point, big business. He saw things that he thought were wrong, and rotten, and the rest is history. He was the leader of the antitrust legislation that took place in this country."

ABC's "Business World" • *November 6, 1988*

❑

❑

Ross-isms

"It was right before [Winston Churchill's] death. All of England was excited because the old man was about to make another speech... Once he got to the podium, he just stood there. Everybody thought he had forgot what he wanted to say. Then, finally, he leaned forward and said, 'Never give in. Never give in. Never. Never. Never.' Now that's a speech."

The Dallas Morning News • *June 28, 1981*

❑

"A man is never more on trial than in a moment of excessive good fortune."

Personal Selling Power • *January-February, 1987*

❑

"I don't go spend much time analyzing myself. I'm just what my family taught me to be, and I'm not nearly everything my family tried to teach me."

Dallas Times Herald • *September 4, 1983*

❑

Each of us acquires pet sayings—pithy one- or two-liners that sum up our attitudes and even our histories. Those uttered by the very successful tend to take on a larger-than-life quality.

The loquacious Perot, who credits the founding of EDS to a Thoreauvian thought—"The mass of men lead lives of quiet desperation"—has himself become a pretty mean coiner of aphorisms. Are they insightful or merely gnomic? Inspirational or dripping with piney woods sappiness?

Judge for yourself in the following sample of 26, which are presented chronologically.

❑

"When I'm an old man, I hope I'll be measured by what kind of children I've raised."

The Dallas Morning News, January 11, 1970

❑

"The man I worry about is the one who hasn't taken any stand."

Time • January 12, 1970

❑

"Failures are like skinned knees—painful but superficial."

Look • March 24, 1970

❑

"There ain't many hunters left, but everybody still wants the meat."

The Dallas Morning News • October 12, 1972

❑

In January of 1979, prior to launching his Iranian rescue mission:

"If you go through life worrying about all the bad things that can happen, you soon convince yourself that it's best to do nothing at all."

Ken Follett's "On Wings of Eagles"

❑

"You just hang in there and stand your ground and don't give an inch and, if you have the will to do that, at some point the tide will turn. If you are wrong, you are just wearing yourself out. If you're right, the tide will turn."

The Dallas Morning News • June 28, 1981

❑

"Now, I'm saying let's assume you've got the goose that lays the golden egg. Then I would study that goose and say, 'How can I get him to lay two?' Not, 'Should we have him for Thanksgiving dinner?'"

CBS's "60 Minutes" • April 1, 1973

❑

"I don't think anybody who knows me thinks I'm too good to be true."

Dallas Times Herald • September 4, 1983

❑

"We may tend to mistake data for wisdom, just as there has been a tendency to confuse logic with values and intelligence with insight."

The Dallas Morning News • September 27, 1983

❑

"[R]emember that life is not orderly. In many cases, life is not logical. Business and life do not follow the neat lines of an organization chart. Both business and life are far more like a cobweb."

EDS booklet • 1984

❑

"Unless I wholeheartedly believe in a cause, I don't get behind it. I'm not interested. But my motto is, 'Once you decide to do something, do it with focus and perseverance.'"

The Dallas Morning News • June 29, 1984

❑

"Success is like Halley's comet, you know. Every now and then it just comes around."

Dallas Times Herald • February 9, 1986

❑

"Your country is like your children. It's fundamentally important that you love them, but you need to work on any problems that come along."

The Dallas Morning News • June 29, 1986

❑

"If your kids grow up living in fairyland thinking that they're princes and princesses, you're going to curse their lives."

Fortune • September 29, 1986

❑

"As a large [GM] stockholder and director, I'm looking for results—I'm not looking for love."

Ward's Auto World • November, 1986

❑

"Inventories can be managed, but people must be led."

Newsweek • December 15, 1986

❑

"Get up in the morning and look in the mirror. You're your own job security."

Personal Selling Power • January-February, 1987

❑

"Our children should be vaccinated and revaccinated with the Bill of Rights and its meaning."

Dallas Times Herald • February 24, 1987

❑

"When you're going to get in fights, you don't give out your game plan."

Dallas Times Herald • May 17, 1987

❑

"The greatest legacy we can leave our children is to develop their intellects fully."

Dallas Times Herald • *November 1, 1987*

❑

"I've made it a point never to learn my social security number because I'm a person, not a number."

Life • *February 1988*

❑

"Anyone who needs a chauffeur to drive him to work is probably too old to be on the payroll."

Fortune • *March 14, 1988*

❑

On management:

"Give 'em more. Constantly give 'em more. Just keep them in a little over their heads. But don't drown 'em. The best ones are like cork. They have a lot of resiliency."

Inc. • *January, 1989*

❑

"Most of you haven't married yet, so here's my advice. Be careful. Be sure. If you're not sure, just hold off a while. It's kind of like buses, there's another one by every 15 minutes, and you can have a lot of fun looking."

Commencement address, Austin College • 1989

❑

"When I get too old to drive to work, I'll quit going."

Fortune • July 16, 1990

❑

"The thing we lack in this country more than anything is Churchill's dictum: 'Action this day.'"

The New York Times • January 27, 1991

5

No Way. (Way?)

❑

Since shortly before embarking on his vain relief flight to North Vietnam in December of 1969, Ross Perot has been viewed as a potential political candidate (admiringly by some, skeptically by others).

Art Garfunkel's ex-partner once found 50 ways to leave a lover. Perot found at least these 34 ways to say he wasn't interested.

Until, that is, the night of February 20, 1992.

❑

"No. I'm too active. What made me a success in business would make me a failure as a politician."

Los Angeles Times • *November 27, 1969*

❑

"I'd be terrible in public office. I'm too action-oriented, which means if I had an idea on Friday and wanted it done by Monday it would be just too much to expect from the government."

Newsweek • *December 8, 1969*

"I don't have any ambitions at all to run for office or to accept an appointed position.

"It would be very difficult, almost impossible for me to accept a public position, because I would have to sell my holdings."

Responded Ted Koppel, then ABC's Hong Kong bureau chief, "In other words, you won't make a Sherman-like statement, you still leave that 'almost' in there?"

"No. Excuse me. I make as Sherman-like a statement as you can phrase for me. I am not going to run for anything, I am not going to be appointed to anything, but as a private citizen I will do everything I can to help this country."

ABC's "Issues and Answers" • January 11, 1970

❑

"I would make a very bad politician. I have no patience for the red tape and inactivity."

New York Sunday News • February 22, 1970

❑

"Once those [POWs] are out, I'm going back to the computer business and you're not going to see anything of me in public again."

New York Daily News • March 14, 1970

"People think I've got political ambitions or am making money out of [the POW issue]. I'm not going to run for anything. I don't think I'd make a good public official. I wouldn't take an appointive job, I'm too impatient. I think I can do more for the country as a private citizen."

Look • March 24, 1970

❑

"Only in a time of national crisis, and then I'd do my duty."

Business Week • May 26, 1973

❑

"This country has enough trouble without having me in office. Seriously, I am not qualified for the job by background, experience or temperament."

Los Angeles Times • August 13, 1980

❑

After agreeing to lead Texas' War on Drugs:
"I am not and will not be a candidate for anything. The last thing I would do is trade off the children of Texas to run for public office."

The Dallas Morning News • February 18, 1981

"I would never run for office. I am not going to run for office. If I could think of a stronger way to say it, I'll say it that way."

The Dallas Morning News • June 28, 1981

❑

To a United Press International reporter in 1985:
"I'd make a terrible politician. My orientation toward results would get me in deep, deep trouble. I have no patience."

The Washington Post • March 29, 1992

❑

Regarding a Lee Iacocca-Perot presidential ticket in 1988:
"Boy, they think they have controversy now... Between the two of us, that'd be one way to get President Reagan off the front pages.

"Between the two of us, we'd stir up more trouble than we could ever solve. Poor old [ABC newsman] Sam Donaldson would probably spin out and turn into an ash in 30 days."

Wall Street Journal • December 9, 1986

❑

"Positions and titles aren't important to me. Results are."

Time • December 15, 1986

❑

After a particularly rousing 1987 speech to the National Governors' Association:
"When people ask what are you going to run for, you say, 'The city limits.' Since 1968 there have been all these theories that I was running for this, that or the other. This country has enough problems without inflicting me on it."

The New York Times • March 1, 1987

❑

"My mother used to say, 'Ross, a little bit of you goes a long way.' I guess quite a few people today would agree. That's why I'd be no good at politics in this laid-back, cool world of television. I'd be too hot. I could never take opinion polls to find out what to think. I like to grapple with what has to be done, not figure out some feel-good campaign."

Life • February 1988

❑

"I think I'd be a fish out of water unless there was a crisis around."

Dallas Times Herald • *November 18, 1988*

❑

"It's not for me. Too much media—I'd rather put asphalt in potholes than call a press conference to discuss them."

Fortune • *July 3, 1989*

❑

"Well, I think it's—my job in life is to create jobs. And I think it's important—see, I might want to play on a professional basketball team. But that wouldn't be playing to my strengths.

"I think people in public and political life operate at a totally different pace, and I am assuming that they have to because that's what the system requires."

PBS's "American Interests" • *September 16, 1989*

❑

"I'd rather stay outside the tent and raise Cain on things like this that need to be done."

The Dallas Morning News • *December 7, 1990*

On Bill Moyers' suggestion, the previous night, that Perot work to establish himself as a Democratic presidential nominee in 1992:

"No. No, I'm a businessman."

CNN's "Larry King Live" • March 19, 1991

❑

In early November of 1991, in the wake of the check-bouncing "Rubbergate" scandal in the House of Representatives, Perot spoke at a Tampa rally for a non-partisan group called THRO (Throw the Hypocritical Rascals Out). Newsweek's report of the appearance was accompanied by a rhetorical question about his political ambitions:

"The answer is no. We can cover that in one word. There's no chance.

"I don't see a scenario that would cause me to change my mind. I don't think running for president or being president plays to my strengths.

"I don't want to be driven around in a motorcade, and I don't want to be led around by the Secret Service. I don't need the ego stroke of a title. I don't want people playing 'Hail to the Chief' every time I go somewhere."

The Dallas Morning News • November 16, 1991

❑

"No. No interest, don't want to be president."

CNN's "Inside Business" • January 5, 1992

❑

"I speak out on the issues. Unfortunately, nowadays if you speak out on the issues, people assume that you're running for something."

Dallas Observer • February 13, 1992

❑

On "Larry King Live," about 40 minutes before Perot began to inflate his trial balloon:

"There's some wonderful people in this country who ought to be running who are not. I wish they would run. They could make a tremendous contribution now."

CNN's "Larry King Live" • February 20, 1992

❑

6

If You Build It, He Will Run

❑

"I can live in the bunker forever. I can just pull the covers over my head like Howard Hughes did and Paul Getty and people with money finally do. But they didn't have any fun. I'm going to do what I want to do and take the licks that go with it."

The Dallas Morning News • *June 28, 1981*

❑

"I thought for a minute, and I said, 'Well, I wanted to be a beautiful pearl,' but I looked in the mirror and decided that wasn't in the cards. And then I said, 'Oh, well, maybe I can be an oyster, because the oyster makes the beautiful pearl.' And that never did work out either. Now, unfortunately, my lot in life is that of the grain of sand that irritates the oyster."

ABC's "20/20" • *April 3, 1986*

❑

"I finally said, 'Look, there's one scenario and only one scenario under which I'd run. If ordinary people in 50 states went out in the streets on their own initiative, not programmed, not orchestrated like rabbits the way we try to do everything now—did it on their own and put me on the ballot in all 50 states, not 48, not 49, but 50—then I would run.'"

Speech to the National Press Club • March 18, 1992

On February 20, 1992, Perot wrote the first chapter of "Field of Presidential Dreams" with his announcement, which came at the tail end of a one-hour guest shot on CNN's "Larry King Live."

What followed seemed like an update of a Frank Capra movie: banks of 1-800 telephones set up overnight and state-by-state committees organizing on the fly. So powerful was the initial surge that no one blinked when it was acknowledged in April that this populist prairie fire was being fanned from above (of the $457,633.42 raised in the first month post-King, $409,823.77 had come from the un-candidate himself).

Offered major exposure on TV shows and newsmagazine covers, Perot accepted—and found himself in closer quarters than he was accustomed to with the media. He has watched journalism's reach grow with every technological advance from radio to television to satellite-fed cable channels dedicated to news from around the world, around the clock. His history of receiving good press notwithstanding, Perot has regarded reporters with the same ambivalence as those skittish horses he used to break back in East Texas.

❑

"Be careful about picking a fight with people who buy ink by the barrel and paper by the ton."

Ken Follett's "On Wings of Eagles"

❑

"I have an interesting problem as far as the media is concerned. It's not unique to me. It's unique to anyone who has had too much luck. It can be a baseball player or a heavyweight boxer. The media just cannot wait for him to lose one. Losing one is bigger news than winning one. You follow me? That's just human nature. It's beyond the media. It's just human nature."

The Dallas Morning News • June 28, 1981

❑

"I only wish that it became good business for the entertainment industry to go patriotic. The current trend in schools and elsewhere to feel apologetic for teaching the people the values of our country might change. Maybe even television comedians, with all their influence, might show some love of country."

The Saturday Evening Post • *April, 1983*

❑

"I think you were dwarfs and wimps in the [1988 presidential] campaign. You let the politicians get away with murder."

Dallas Times Herald • *November 18, 1988*

❑

"I called my friends on network television [after the 1988 presidential campaign]. I said, 'Why don't you guys make them face the issues?' And they said, 'This is all they will give us.' And I said, 'Let me give you a cure to that. Just put them off the air for a day or two because free TV time to a politician is like oxygen—and then they will talk to you about the issues.'"

PBS's "American Interests" • *September 16, 1989*

❑

"The day you see me with a PR man and a sound bite or spin control, hell is frozen over! What you see is what you get."

"Donahue" • *January 8, 1991*

For a man said to prickle under criticism, Perot had usually resisted lashing out at the media. One exception came in the late 1980s, when Dallas' minority communities and the police were deeply divided. After three cops were shot in January of 1988, Perot weighed in with his support for the men in blue.

On March 13 of that year, Dallas Times Herald columnist Laura Miller wrote: "[Perot] has ideas about how the police department should operate... He has discussed them in off-the-record meetings held with 29 newspaper, TV and radio people. He has told me about them in five separate telephone interviews... Perot came up with a solution. Pick a night for a covert operation and cordon off a section of South Dallas. Send hundreds of police officers—however many it would take—into the area to 'vacuum it up.' Shake down everybody on the street. Search every house and apartment. Confiscate all drugs and weapons."

Perot went ballistic as he rarely had in public.

"While most of these damn liberals in Dallas sit around and suck their thumbs and wring their hands, who paid for [a food bank for the needy]? I paid for the damn warehouse. Who does the mayor call when there's no place to put homeless people, to build the shelter? She calls me, and I paid for the damn thing.

"It bothers me a lot to have spent 20 years of my life and tens of millions of dollars trying to help the minorities in this state and get the kind of reaction I'm getting now. I never expect anybody to thank me, and nobody ever did. But I sure as hell didn't expect to get my teeth kicked in (and be called) a racist."

Dallas Times Herald • March 16, 1988

When Perot commented on the Miller column again in 1992, seven weeks into his un-candidacy, he was far less combative.

"I did not say it, and it was just one of those unfortunate things that got into print."

The Dallas Morning News • April 11, 1992

Still, it didn't take long for campaign-trail reporters to settle like burrs on the Texan's chaps. Even as Perot's polls soared, the questions began getting more nettlesome. Barely had Oscar winner Jack Palance completed his one-arm push-ups when the detente began dissolving.

❑

"Unfortunately, [Washington] has become a town filled with sound bites, shell games, handlers and media stuntmen, who posture, create images and talk, shoot off Roman candles, but don't ever accomplish anything. If they want to debate that, I'll buy my own television time."

Speech to the National Press Club • March 18, 1992

On the intense press scrutiny:

"It's just part of the process. I consider part of it is really off the screen now. I think the tabloids are starting to look more and more respectable because of the way we tear at our public officials' lives. I have thought that through. And, again, where I have come out, when you look at where I started in this life and when you look at where I am now, and as lucky as I've been, I have an obligation if the people want me to do this and that includes all of the stuff that goes with it."

PBS's "MacNeil/Lehrer NewsHour" • March 26, 1992

❑

"The more I'm in it, the less interesting it becomes.

"[But] there are worse things in life than this."

The Dallas Morning News • April 11, 1992

❑

"If we're going to spend all morning looking for hidden agendas, then you're just burning up my time and yours."

The New York Times • April 13, 1992

❑

"Nothing ever comes up that's relevant to the issues. Pretty soon, people are going to want to know how many mosquitoes I have in my house."

The Dallas Morning News • *April 18, 1992*

❑

"Now, they have a theory that I'm thin-skinned. I love their theory. Just hang onto it fellas, you keep using it. Anybody that even takes a casual glance at my life will conclude that I am the reverse of thin-skinned—that if I believe in something I will not be detracted from what needs to be done by what I call silly little stray bullets."

PBS's "Talking With David Frost" • *April 24, 1992*

❑

"I'll probably issue position papers because I've got a good sense of humor. [The media] will be more interested in what I eat for breakfast or my hair style."

Boston Globe • *April 24, 1992*

❑

"My least favorite thing is to be sound-bitten."

Business Week • *April 27, 1992*

❑

"Maybe there is a Pulitzer Prize here if you could say this dumb bastard in Texas wants to take money from old folks. Now I'm not there yet. But I'll tell you this, if I ever get there, I'll talk about it."

The Washington Post • May 3, 1992

❑

"If you ever see me doing photo opportunities, have me led away. Just put on the front page of your paper, 'This guy has lost it.'"

The Washington Post • May 5, 1992

❑

"Night and day there is saturation bombing; there are Patriot missiles going down airshafts in my office. All you good reporters wanting to know my positions on everything from mosquitoes to ants."

The New York Times • May 6, 1992

❑

On continuing media probes:

"These stories typically have a very positive effect on the petition signing drive and causing people to want to rally around.

"So I guess I should get up every morning and say, 'Hit me, please.'"

The New York Times • May 16, 1992

❑

Yet, Perot began to cut back on his press appearances. One reason, he said, was to give himself 60 days to consult with experts and advisors; after backgrounding himself on unfamiliar issues, he would make known his stands.

A Matter of Opinion

"I will not sound-bite complex issues."

The Dallas Morning News • March 26, 1992

❑

Perot and his advisors were confronted with the rapid emergence in American culture of single-issue politics. Not very long ago, national candidates had only to woo key voting blocs like organized labor and large ethnic and religious groups. Today, the litmus tests have multiplied into a dazzling and dizzying gamut of political correctness exams.

Perot had been trying to play catch-up ball on some of the issues he will be forced to address. On others, though, he was far from a cipher. The following passages—arranged by themes, beginning with domestic issues—show him to be, for instance, a long-time advocate of improved race relations, but most likely not Planet Earth's best friend.

Blacks and whites in America

On racism in 1930s Texarkana:
"White people didn't go into black people's homes, but [my father] did. Every black person who worked for him carried his business card in case they were ever rudely treated by the police or anybody else."

U.S. News & World Report • June 20, 1988

❑

"Every person in this country should have in fact, not just in theory, an equal opportunity."

The New York Times • November 28, 1969

❑

On donating $1 million to expand the Boy Scouts into Dallas' impoverished ethnic neighborhoods:
"Scouting has been for the white middle class. We could develop a whole new youth program but it might take 10 years to be effective nationally. In Scouting, you can do it overnight."

New York Daily News • February 22, 1970

❑

On the civil rights legislation of the 1960s, when asked, "Do you think Negroes are demanding too much?":

"Let's say minorities. There are others besides Negroes. I would like to deliver to every man the guarantees of the Constitution... there are some among the minorities who are demanding too much."

New York Daily News • February 22, 1970

❑

"School can become the best part of a disadvantaged or minority child's life, because there's so little good happening in that child's life, if we do that part right, that can become the spark that gives that child a chance to be someone."

ABC's "Business World" • January 31, 1988

❑

On a quota system for hiring federal employees:
"We'd spend a lot of time discussing that before we made a decision. And the reason is the quota system now produces stress between the races, and if you take a less qualified person because of his background or color and promote him over a more qualified person, you create stress. There are reasons for the origin of the quota system."

CNN's "Evans and Novak" • April 11, l992

❑

Perot in the mid-1980s, quoted by Philadelphia civil rights minister Leon Sullivan:
"If Mandela being in jail is the problem, let's find a way to get him out."

The New York Times • April 27, 1992

❑

On racial divisions, two weeks after the beating in Los Angeles of black motorist Rodney King by white policemen:
"The military is an example for our country on getting rid of racism. It is a terrible blight on our country that we still have it—and this thing that happened in Los Angeles [the Rodney King incident] is a heart-breaker—but it's there. When I say jobs, I mean jobs for everybody. Everybody fought, everybody ought to have an opportunity. Historically, the minorities don't get the same breaks the rest get. Straight down the board, color-blind, just like the military. Follow that example."

CNN's "Larry King Live" • March 19, 1991

❑

On Rodney King, one year later:
"The videotape is just inescapable evidence of brutality."

The Washington Post • May 3, 1992

On the ensuing Los Angeles riots:
"The first thing I'd do [as president] is head for the airport to go to Los Angeles, because that is a sad thing that just breaks this country apart."

The Washington Post • May 3, 1992

❑

"If I could capture all the energy we lose in racial division I could light up this country with it."

The New York Times • May 13, 1992

❑

Immigration

"We just can't have people coming in here willy-nilly. Frankly, it's touching that they want to come so badly they'll cross the border illegally and endure many hardships. But it has to be legal. We, as a nation, have to make it a conscious decision."

Dallas Times Herald • September 18, 1985

❑

"Highly productive immigrants that were oppressed built this country.

"When we finally got to the point where we couldn't figure out what to do, on more than one occasion—transcontinental railroad, Chinese got us through the mountains. Panama Canal, the Chinese got us through the big cut.

"Then you have a nonproductive segment of our population that we must address, and we must talk about, and we must make productive, and you're right back to the public schools. And you can't just funnel them through the middle class school system. You've got to give them the education."

PBS's "American Interests" • September 16, 1989

❑

American Jews and Israel

"The best way to solve [Saddam Hussein's invasion of Kuwait] is to let the Arabs work it out. We must protect Israel. But the Arabs will shift the sand around, work something out, come up with some new puzzle that we can barely perceive and we will have some stability in the Middle East. "

"Donahue" • January 8, 1991

❑

"Israel is our friend, and you stand by your friends. It's just that simple."

The New York Times • May 13, 1992

❑

On being asked if he belonged to a club that excluded Jews and blacks:

"Yes, I do. And I go there about once a year. And all my Jewish friends in Dallas, they've had a great deal of fun with me over this. If if bothers the people, I will quit immediately.

"But I have to tell you this story. So my Jewish pals one day gave me a mezuzah as a gift and they said, 'Now you can put this on your door, Perot,' and I said, 'Well, which door?' They said, 'Any door you want to.' And this was all in great spirit, as you can imagine. So a few days go by and they come back to me. They all know that maybe once a year I'll go down there for a lunch or something like that. I don't play golf, don't have a golf locker. They all know that...

"[They] come back in a few days and say, 'Perot, have you put your mezuzah up?' and I say, 'Yes, it's up.' They say, 'Where did you put it?' I say, 'I've got it on my locker door at the country club,' and they all say, 'My gosh, Perot, they'll throw you out!' I say, 'No, nobody knows what it is.'

"I could have resigned the day before and given a politically-correct answer. I haven't. It's never been a point of stress with all of my friends across the spectrum—blacks, whites, browns, Jews, and what-have-you."

CNN's "Larry King Live" • April 16, 1992

Gender issues

On legal abortions:
"I think this is the woman's decision. God knows what kind of demonstrations I'll have outside my office now."

Speech to the National Press Club • March 18, 1992

❑

On permitting the federal funding of abortions:
"Haven't spent ten minutes to think about it.

"There's far more to it than just the woman's choice. We are not rabbits. We are thinking, reasoning human beings. And every human life is precious. And thinking, reasoning human beings ought to act responsibly not to create human lives they don't want...

"See, we do not have to create human life if we don't want to. And we shouldn't create a human life if we don't want to. And every little human life is precious. So, let's take a little responsibility in our lives."

CNN's "Evans and Novak" • April 11, 1992

❑

"Let's go to the creation of a human life, and I've said this a thousand times... There are all kinds of ways for people to have relations and not create a human life. Now I consider it irresponsible, and this is just plain sailor-Texas talk, to get drunk, get high, get laid, get pregnant. You are not taking responsibility for creating this precious human life."

PBS's "Talking With David Frost" • April 24, 1992

❑

On non-discriminatory business practices:
"Women—let's get specific—absolutely women, in my experience, are more talented than men. So my biggest problem in my computer companies is they keep getting married and leaving me. But in terms of, did they contribute to building [the companies]? Yes. Were they treated as equal? Yes. I had a woman director at a point in time when it was considered so odd that they ran a full-page story in a national magazine. Why was she a director? She was the best qualified person."

CBS's "Face the Nation" • April 26, 1992

❑

Senior citizen entitlement programs

"Now if you want to really get controversial, just don't give folks that don't need it their Social Security and Medicare. For example, I'd get along all right without mine."

Speech to the National Press Club • March 18, 1992

❑

Law and order

"We do everything in the world to take care of the bad guys, including giving them color television and weight rooms [in jail], and we do everything in the world to cause anybody with any sense to either get out of police work or stop doing their job."

Dallas Times Herald, March 5, 1988

❑

"I'm not a police groupie. I feel strongly that the police officers who risk their lives to defend the law-abiding citizens of this country should have the same constitutional rights and civil rights as the citizens they arrest."

The Dallas Morning News • March 12, 1988

On the white cops who beat Rodney King:
"The thing that just leaped at me was the shock that a group of men could do that. Second, I couldn't believe that the other guys didn't stop it."
The New York Times • May 4, 1992

❑

Homosexuality

"We have supported AIDS research, we have helped raise money for AIDS research. If I am on this job, we will go night and day to get that done. Not only for this country but for the world.

"Now, I just say each person has their individual rights in our country."
PBS's "Talking With David Frost" • April 24, 1992

❑

Gun control

"Now when I was a boy, everybody had guns, but we didn't shoot one another. Now everybody's got guns and they go out and shoot one another...

"The Brady bill is, you register and what have you. Well, the bad guys—that's not going to slow them down 10 minutes. Your big-time dope dealer, you can buy guns from all over the world, right?

"Gun control is a very complex issue, but we've got to think, what is the objective? Get the guns out of the hands of the bad guys. You don't care if people collect guns. You don't care if people have guns for hunting. You care like the devil if somebody's just going to show up on the street and shoot you because he's bored, and that happens in our country now. We've got to fix that and fix it now. That can be fixed, but you can't fix it ducking it and you can't worry about all these powerful lobbies."

Speech to the National Press Club • March 18, 1992

❑

"I don't really care if you keep a Patriot missile in your back yard, if you're a collector, right? I don't care. But if you shoot it, I get worried."

CNN's "Larry King Live" • April 16, 1992

❑

"God bless the honest people in that part of [riot-torn Los Angeles] who live by the rules. If they didn't have a gun, they couldn't survive right now."

The New York Times • May 4, 1992

The environment

On leaving his office to greet 22 environmental activists picketing over a Perot development in Austin, Texas, that was threatening the habitat of the golden-cheeked warbler:

"I share your interest in wildlife.

"If the people of Austin want that land as a park or a bird sanctuary or for any other purpose, I will be happy to sell it to them for what I have in the property."

The Dallas Morning News • July 6, 1986

❑

"Somebody could come in and say, 'What about the gray owl? Let's take that first.' Well, the environment—that's a piece of the endangered species list. But compared to keeping the financial pump going, you can't discuss it because if the financial pump breaks, you don't have any money to take care of the gray owl."

C-SPAN • March 18, 1992

❑

"If we're broke, we can't fix the environment. We have got to rebuild our industrial base."

CNN's "Larry King Live" • April 16, 1992

"I'm pragmatic. If there's a choice between survival and protecting the planet, we will pillage and plunder the planet, if it gets that basic.

"Let's assume you don't have a job and I don't have a job and the only thing we can do is cut every tree in the area and ship it to Japan to feed our children. We're going to want to cut every tree in the area to ship it to Japan to feed our children... Nobody will think about the Spotted Owl if they're starving, except maybe to eat him."

The Washington Post • *May 3, 1992*

❑

Perot tends to speak of the nations that lie beyond America's border in economic terms: Are they competitive? Are they stable enough to ensure the safety of the employees of U.S. companies (an understandable concern after the 1979 EDS rescue mission in Tehran)? Are they worth defending by force of arms?

"Oil is the most worthless commodity in the world unless you sell it. If the devil runs the Middle East, he will sell the oil. That's all he's got. He's got camels, scorpions and sand and [a] market for oil.

"Donahue" • *January 8, 1991*

❑

The country in which he has exhibited an interest beyond that of the marketplace is the former Soviet Union.

❑

At the dawn of "glasnost":

"I find it fascinating to watch [Mikhail] Gorbachev these days.

"Now, if you think we have got a consensus problem in this country, once you let the Russian people start criticizing their government and criticizing their officials, once you release all that pent-up energy from all these years when they just had to take whatever was dumped on them—it will be fun to watch Gorbachev in action. Because he could be heading himself for a revolution. I mean when you release all that energy, somehow you have to control all the steam.

"Now, if he can control the steam, he can generate all the electricity in the world. Otherwise, he can get burned. And I think it is going to be fascinating to watch Russia over the next few years."

Barron's • February 23, 1987

❑

"God bless Gorbachev. I don't know what he's doing internationally, but at home he has touched the tarbaby. He is making revolutionary change, and we are standing here like Lawrence Welk saying 'wonderful, wonderful, wonderful'—and it's not."

PBS's "American Interests" • September 16, 1989

❑

As the Iron Curtain was falling:
"This time last year it was Eastern Europe. We were busy with that. Now we are in winter in Russia. Will Gorbachev make it or not, will the people have enough food? We should be totally focused on helping Eastern Europe complete its revolution. No, we have to have a big event and now we are in the Middle East."

PBS's "MacNeil/Lehrer NewsHour" • December 6, 1990

❑

After Boris Yeltsin had succeeded Gorbachev:
"I would love to have a country that could always reach out and help other countries. It is a whole lot cheaper to help Russia right now than it is to have a new cold war pop up in 18 months because we didn't.

"It costs so little to help Russia go from where she is over to a free economy and a stand-alone country, and it costs so much to have her regress because her people are hungry. Now if I were in united Europe, I would really be nervous because, you know, if Russia gets hungry guess where the nearest food is."

CNN's "Larry King Live," • February 20, 1992

❑

"Now, this gets a little technical, and you've got to handle this smoothly, but, see, one of the reasons we're in the spot we're in, we've been defending Asia and Europe out of our pocket. So we go very nicely and diplomatically and positively to our friends in Europe and say, 'Folks, we just can't do it anymore, but if you want to pay us $100 billion a year, we'll be glad to kind of stick around, and, you know, if something pops up, we'll be there.' Go to our friends in Asia. That's another $100 billion. Tell them the same thing. You say, 'Wait a minute, Ross. They'll just shut it down.' Don't be silly. You've got an unstable Russia. You've got a hungry bear, right? Nobody knows what's going to happen in Russia. Only a fool would shut down the ability to keep Europe and Asia stable, because the bear can go two ways."

Speech to the National
Press Club • March 18, 1992

The purpose of issuing white papers, of course, is to spell out the sort of remedies a candidate hopes to apply to problems. Perot promised to make known his positions in early summer of 1992. Even before receiving specifics, though, it was reasonable to conclude that they would stress activism, the A-Team approach he's traditionally applied to solving problems and a strong sense of personal responsibility.

❑

"You know, the Mormon Church requires its young people to give one year of service, and it's called a mission. Well, I endorse that, and our government should have the same requirement: Every young American should go on a mission of service to his or her country.

"At some time in your life, you should give a year or two to your country. I wouldn't call it 'conscription.' I would call it 'Service to Country.' Every 18-year-old could work on jobs like conservation projects, hospital service or helping older people. It would have to have substance and be well organized.

"That young person would come out with an understanding of service, of being less selfish and of people. Finally, that young person would have worked around government and would therefore know what it can do and what its limitations are."

The Saturday Evening Post • *April, 1983*

❑

On tapping executives to revitalize the economy:

"Don't pay them anything. Have them report directly to the president. And have those people put together small teams to come up with plans industry by industry. For example, in the automobile industry, my candidate would be Don Petersen, recently retired chairman of Ford. If you are worried about conflicts of interest, fine. Bring lawyers and economists who don't know and let them put together a plan that will fail."

The Washington Post • *December 22, 1991*

❑

"We have the most expensive health care system in the world, and yet we are behind 15 other nations in life expectancy and behind 22 other nations in infant mortality. So we don't have the finest health care system in the world for our money. Study the nations that have more cost-effective systems. Build pilot projects. Keep the people informed about what the benefits and what the costs are and go to a health care system that does a better job and costs less money."

"Donahue" • *March 24, 1992*

"We would run pilot programs and give the people who are running them complete freedom to optimize them in the pilot phase. You run your pilot programs, come back to the people and give them the results. You might have a plan for rural areas and another for urban areas. You thrash that through. And you tell the people the cost. Then we mass-produce the successful pilot models."

Wall Street Journal • *April 9, 1992*

❑

In Your Face

No matter what the merits of his programs, how would Perot, if elected, persuade 100 Senators and 435 Representatives to enact them into law? After all, not only has he lambasted the legislators for their excesses, but he would also hold no party-line leverage over them.

"Can I work with legislature? That's a good question. Go down and look at the Texas legislature. I worked with them twice—once on drug laws, once on education. There was no confrontation. There was a lot of controversy, any time, but we got it done."

CNN's "Larry King Live" • *April 16, 1992*

"Now, I haven't spent my life up there in politics, but I know how to get things done, and you don't get things done giving orders. You get things done by building consensus."

PBS's "Talking With David Frost" • April 24, 1992

Indeed, on issues he holds dear, Perot has put aside his confrontation-by-wisecrack style.

❑

On the "dissent [that] has developed" against the Vietnam War:

"I don't use the word 'dissenters' because that kind of indicates they are against something they should be for. But anybody that knows what he wants and is working hard to get it within our system, them I am 100 percent for. I don't necessarily have to agree with them. They don't have to agree with me."

ABC's "Issues and Answers" • January 11, 1970

❑

On lobbying for Congressional action on POWs:

"I urge the Congress and the Senate to meet in joint session and spend the better part of one day—I don't mean next fall, I mean in the very near future—hearing from these wives, learning firsthand the plight of these men.

"I would also ask you to do everything in your power to create a yes or no situation where the Congress and the Senate are either willing to give this the necessary time, or they are not.

"If you do meet in joint session, the North Vietnamese at the highest level, knowing the scope and size of events that have historically caused you to meet in joint session, will feel a tremendous amount of pressure."

Testimony before the House Subcommittee and Scientific Developments • May 6, 1970

❑

On his opposition to the controversial Vietnam Veterans Memorial in Washington, D.C., during an appearance with Maya Ying Lin, the architecture student who won the design competition that Perot helped sponsor:

"Well, as far as I'm concerned there's no hatchet to bury. We have one interest here, and that's to make sure that this is a memorial that the men like. I think a key factor at this point is that the 2.5 million men and women who fought in Vietnam take a close look at this memorial and really make their feelings known. If they like it, terrific; if they feel it's inappropriate, this is one time when the Vietnam veterans need to come out of the closet and let the world know where they stand on this memorial."

ABC's "Nightline" • October 14, 1982

Perot now regularly visits the black granite slab on his trips to Washington.

The majority of his opponents, though, have endured far less graciousness than feisty ridicule.

"Go to Austin and sit in on a meeting [of the Texas State Board of Education]. It costs you $5 to see a movie that funny. They got people on that board who think the earth is flat."

The Washington Post • May 31, 1984

❑

"Getting a piece of me is like going to a barbershop on Saturday. You take a ticket and stand in line."

Business Week • October 6, 1986

❑

Perot has often saved his adversaries the trouble by taking the battle directly to them.

To a gathering of bankers:

"I guarantee you the average citizen doesn't understand the banker. I still don't."

The Dallas Morning News, October 12, 1972

At a hearing on Texas educational reforms:

Perot: "I've found little schools that have 60 teachers and 12 coaches."

Principal: "That's rare."

Perot: "So is a one-legged tap-dancer, but it happens."

The Dallas Morning News • September 15, 1983

❑

To 700 school-board members and administrators: "This is the group that let costs go through the roof while academic achievement went through the floor. It starts to seem ludicrous that you want to keep the captain of the ship that ran aground every time you gave him the helm.

"If we're going to look after the children, we've got to put in a team that can manage this system. Sooner or later, the old-boy network has got to break down. You can't throw enough money at this system and make it work. It is a bad system."

The Dallas Morning News • April 19, 1984

❑

From a 1985 letter to General Motors Chairman Roger Smith, demanding that Perot be consulted in GM's proposed $5.2-billion acquisition of Hughes Aircraft: "You need to recognize that I am one of the few people who can and will disagree with you... If you continue your present autocratic style, I will be your adversary on critical issues… Your tendency to try to run over anyone who disagrees with you hurts your effectiveness within GM. You need to know that GM-ers at all levels use terms like 'ruthless' and 'bully' in describing you."

The New York Times • March 26, 1989

❑

To Ronald Reagan in early 1987, after charging that elements in the White House were thwarting Perot's mission to locate MIAs in Southeast Asia:
"Mr. President, is this how you want to go down in the history books? Even if it's a hundred years from now, do you want people to read that you did nothing to bring them home?"

Monika Jensen-Stevenson and William Stevenson's "Kiss the Boys Goodbye"

❑

To 200 Washington, D.C.-area business leaders:
"The point is, how can you live with having one of the worst school systems in the nation?

"Get out of your fancy house. Get down there where the rubber meets the road… and say, 'Let's fix this; let's help these folks.'"

Dallas Times Herald • March 29, 1989

To corporate and government leaders at a speech sponsored by the Securities and Exchange Commission:

"Even in a bad year, the Who's Who of corporate America grants themselves enormous bonuses. It is obscene to have the gap between the factory floor and the corner office that we have."

The New York Times • March 30, 1992

❑

To America:

"If voters don't have a stomach for me, they can get one of those blow-dried guys."

Time • April 6, 1992

❑

Bush-Whacker

"Public officials should talk to the people more and explain their programs. If a program can't be explained, it's a pretty bad program."

New York Daily News • February 22, 1970

❑

"Right after the [1988] election, I said publicly that as far as I was concerned, the candidates weren't dwarfs and wimps, the American people were—because we never forced them to face the issues during the campaign. We got flag factory tours, tank trips—the most silly things in the world."

PBS's "American Interests" • September 16, 1989

❑

"We've got a patient whose heart has stopped beating and has broken fingers and toes, and all the politicians want to talk about is the fingers and toes. I want to go straight to the heart."

The New York Times • March 29, 1992

❑

Perot has never been one to hide his light under a 10-gallon hat. Yet moving into 1600 Pennsylvania Avenue without benefit of major-party affiliation seems an audacious ambition even for him.

The exact sequence of thoughts, experiences and emotions he carried into Larry King's studio on the evening of February 20, 1992—the combustibles that triggered his announcement—will be exhaustively analyzed in the in-depth biographies of the future.

But a study of Perot's public concerns since the last general election reveals a heightening frustration with the splintering of America. And he has publicly laid the responsibility at the doors of the nation's leaders, both corporate and government.

None has received as much scorn as the sitting President.

On advice he would give George Bush:
"I'd get rid of handlers. I say, why worry about your image? Why don't you worry about what you're doing instead?"

Management Review • *June, 1990*

❑

"Why don't our leaders give domestic problems priority? It's pretty simple: They're controversial, they're difficult to resolve. Now, it's really exciting to jet all over the world for one or two days meeting with heads of state. It's exciting to watch until you realize it's not producing anything for us. So I'd like for everyone to come home and go to work."

The Dallas Morning News • *December 7, 1990*

❑

On Bush's "New World Order":
"It's a sound bite. It doesn't mean anything. I would buy an hour on television to have somebody explain what it is."

"Donahue" • *January 8, 1991*

❑

"You know, we've got the same guy working with the President that created Don Trump's image.

Now, how's that? Only in America. Well, anyway—he's a guy out of Las Vegas. I wish my President didn't have image makers, but he does."

CNN's "Larry King Live" • January 11, 1991

❑

"We're approaching the 1992 election. The economy's still in a slump. We'll do what we did in 1988. Think of a great old race horse with sore legs. Just before the election, we'll get the horse out of the barn, shoot up its legs with painkillers and hope that we can win one more race."

The New York Times • November 5, 1991

They both claim Texas citizenship, but Perot lives there while the President calls a hotel in Houston his primary residence, saving him some $59,000 in 1991 state income taxes he would otherwise have had to pay to Maine. One is short, the other tall. One went to a junior college and then a service academy, the other to a prep school and an Ivy League college. One has always relished the role of entrepreneur, the other has always prided himself on international public service.

Dallas and Washington may be separated by 1,300 miles, but over the decades, the paths of Perot and Bush, both registered Republicans, often crossed. So did their swords, by one account, over the issue of MIAs.

At the time Iran-contra was breaking in late 1986-

early 1987, Perot had obtained White House clearance to review classified intelligence on whether there were still Americans alive and captive in Southeast Asia. Then-Vice President Bush inquired about his progress.

"Well, George, I go in looking for prisoners, but I spend all my time discovering the government has been moving drugs around the world and is involved in illegal arms deals... I can't get at the prisoners because of the corruption among our own covert people."

Monika Jensen-Stevenson and William Stevenson's "Kiss the Boys Goodbye"

The Stevensons write that Bush (who headed the CIA for two years in the mid-1970s) later informed his fellow Texan that Perot's access to the files had been revoked.

After Bush was elected to the White House, Perot's criticisms of the new administration were focused mostly on policy matters until Iraq invaded Kuwait on August 2, 1990. The closer America drifted toward armed conflict, the more scornful Perot grew about presidential priorities.

"The worst mistake we have made is personalizing war: 'I have had it with Hussein.' I have never heard anybody talk about war in the first person. If we are going to have a first-person fight we will get [boxing promoter] Don King to arrange it, have it in Atlantic City and get it over with between [these] two people."

PBS's "MacNeil/Lehrer NewsHour" • December 6, 1990

❑

"I've watched Secretary [of State James] Baker on C-Span until I can't take it anymore, saying that the lesson of Vietnam is to use overwhelming force. He missed it, I'm sorry.

"First commit the nation, then commit the troops. That is the lesson of Vietnam."

The Dallas Morning News • December 7, 1990

❑

On Bush's emerging coalition against Saddam Hussein:

"Guess what, we found a new bad boy down the block, [Hafez] Assad of Syria. I never dreamed my country would walk in the room and have a meeting with the man who blew up the marines in Lebanon and blew up [Pan Am Flight] 103 [over Lockerbie, Scotland]. I cannot believe that we have done that but it has been done."

PBS's "MacNeil/Lehrer NewsHour" • December 6, 1990

On Bush's willingness to project military force:
"Last year, Panama was the front-page news, right? Go to Panama today. We abandoned Panama right after we took it. The people are still living in tents. They're destitute. We didn't finish what we started.

"You think the same amateur crowd that couldn't handle Nicaragua and Panama can suddenly do the Middle East? I'm sorry. They can't."

"Donahue" • January 8, 1991

❑

On how Bush's diplomacy helped precipitate Saddam's invasion:
"Now, you can just track it right on up, but let's come down to July 25th, 1990. [U.S. Ambassador to Iraq April] Glaspie goes in to see Hussein with written instructions from the Secretary of State, approved by the President of the United States: 'We will not become involved in your border dispute with Kuwait and we take no position on this dispute.' In plain talk, they're saying, 'You can take the northern part of the country and you can take the islands. We won't do anything.'

"The Emir [of Kuwait] is not the American way of life—70 wives, seven personal 747's, half the oil that comes out of the ground goes into his pocket. I work second shift, live in a little house in the Midwest. The apple of my eye is over there. Do you think I want to lose my son for this guy? No."

CNN's "Larry King Live" • January 11, 1991

As of May 16, 1992, that communiqué to Ambassador Glaspie remained classified.

The swift prosecution of the Gulf War failed to silence Perot, nor did victory.

❑

"We will lunge at these international problems, but we have stopped trying to solve domestic issues. Let's say you're President and you're concerned about rape, plunder, and pillage. You don't have to go to Iraq; you can find it in New York, Detroit and Chicago."

The New York Times • January 27, 1991

❑

"I would suggest that if we don't like brutal Third World dictators, then we shouldn't help create another. And we have a pattern here. We traded Noriega. We had to get rid of [Saddam]. For 10 years, we supported his side. We sent him weapons, we sent him billions of dollars, got out of control, we had to get rid of him. Now we've embraced Assad of Syria.

"I would hope the one lesson we would learn is Churchill's simple phrase, 'Never cozy up with tyrants. They'll always turn on you.'"

PBS's "MacNeil/Lehrer NewsHour" • March 14, 1991

❑

"Well, let's net it out. Our objectives were to get Saddam Hussein—his nuclear, chemical, bacteriological capability. It's all still intact."

CNN's "Larry King Live," • February 20, 1992

❑

"Let's put a turbine under all this [post-war] euphoria and use it to clean up our problems over here. One success will not carry anybody very far. We need to put it behind us and press forward. If we just sit around and high-five one another over the fact that we blew the bejesus out of the Arab world, nothing but arrogance can come out of it."

The New York Times, March 4 • 1991

❑

"Saddam Hussein is still alive and not so well, probably, but he's still floating around up there.

"I certainly don't mean to suggest that we should risk our men on the battlefield to go to

Baghdad to get him, but he's still loose. He's like a phoenix... He's got oil. He can come out of the ashes over time if we're not careful.

"We won the war. We haven't won the peace. Let's make sure we draw the line on that.

"More people were murdered violently in Washington, D.C., between August 2nd [of 1990] and the end of the war than were killed on and off the battlefield. So we've got work right here to do."

PBS's "MacNeil/Lehrer NewsHour" • March 14, 1991

❑

"Look how good we feel. Why do we feel good?

"Because the big gorilla whipped a midget."

CNN's "Larry King Live" • March 19, 1991

❑

"We rescued the Emir of Kuwait. Now if I knock on your door and say I'd like to borrow your son to go to the Middle East so that this dude with 70 wives, who's got a minister for sex to find him a virgin every Thursday night, can have his throne back, you'd probably hit me in the mouth."

C-Span • March 23, 1992

❑

"Isn't it bizarre that the only heroes from this war are generals and politicians?"

The Christian Science Monitor • March 24, 1992

Desert Storm and the implosion of the Soviet empire did little in 1991 to alleviate America's economic slump. Coupled with a string of inside-the-Beltway follies—check-kiting Congressmen, senior White House aides using government planes for private trips—Perot found himself back on his home turf, poking the cows he knew so well.

❑

On Congress, at a late-1991 rally in Tampa, Fla., for THRO (Throw the Hypocritical Rascals Out):

"It's time somebody cleaned out the barn.

"Unless the average citizen gets upset, that three-act comedy up there is going to continue."

The Dallas Morning News • November 3, 1991

❑

"These people work for you and me, but they don't act like our servants. Close the barber shop, the gym, the parking lot. Make them pay for it. Ground every airplane for Federal officials except Air Force One. Let 'em fly commercial, get in line, wait three hours, get their baggage lost. We're going broke, and they're flying around in our airplanes."

The New York Times • November 5, 1991

❑

"The inventor of the integrated circuit lives in Dallas, Texas, a great guy, Dr. Jack Kelbit, [but] 19 out of 20 integrated circuits used in the United States are made in Japan. Most of that happened because of sheer stupidity between government and business and the fact that we allow foreign lobbyists to come into our country, pour hundreds of millions of dollars a year into political campaigns and tilt the deck.

"I'll give you one example. The Japanese spent $3 million one time and got trucks declared cars coming into the country. Lowered the import rate from 25 percent to two-and-a-half percent. Once they got on the lot they got them redeclared trucks so they didn't have to pay emission penalty and low-mileage penalty.

"I'd like to have one person try to explain that—they can't."

CNN's "Inside Business, Pt. 1" • January 5, 1992

❑

"Quit talking about it. Quit posturing. Quit soundbiting. Quit running all over the country every night and throwing rocks at one another. 'You know it's all the Democrats' fault. No, it's all the Republicans' fault.' I'd like to get them all in a room and say, 'Listen, stupid, you work for us.'"

CNN's "Inside Business, Pt. 2" • January 5, 1992

❑

In late 1991, Perot's son, Big Ross, made a modest contribution to the Bush re-election campaign. Shortly thereafter, Bush announced that he was taking a group of American leaders of industry on his long-planned trip to visit Pacific Rim trading partners.

"Why should the President take all of these businessmen around the world with him? If those businessmen worked for me, I'd say, 'Listen suckers. We got problems. Don't be wandering around the world going to parties and receptions with the president. Let's get out here in the field and fix our problems. This trip is nothing more than an election year media stunt.'"

The Washington Post • December 22, 1991

❑

"Somebody up there needs to understand that talking about problems doesn't fix a thing. Somebody up there better pick up a shovel and go out there and start cleaning up the barn.

"To show you how corrupt the system is, at first we had 'Watch my lips, no new taxes,' right? Then we had the tax and budget summit which was a study in arrogance, the White House and Congress fighting with one another. They should be holding hands, working together for the benefit of the American people."

CNN's "Inside Business" • January 5, 1992

❑

"I think the President taking [U.S. executives] with him on this trip was a serious mistake. I'm appalled that people who supposedly understand diplomacy would show up with 21 uninvited guests.

"The problems we have, [the Japanese] can't cure for us. It was a counterproductive trip, and not in our nation's interest.

"This trip was just a joke."

Wall Street Journal • January 13, 1992

❑

"In all candor, I don't think he understands it. He's interested in international affairs—doesn't understand business; doesn't like to work on domestic issues. I think he realizes now he's got to get into it."

CNN's "Larry King Live," • February 20, 1992

Toward the end of that show, Perot allowed that if he were petitioned onto the ballots of all 50 states, he would wage a run for the Oval Office. Even before his candidacy was formally declared, he was ignoring the Democratic contenders to take dead aim on the certain Republican ticket.

❑

"The chief financial officer of a publicly owned corporation would be sent to prison if he kept books like our government...

"We cannot continue to tolerate this. The average citizen works five months a year just to pay his taxes. Forty-two percent of his income goes to taxes. All the personal income taxes collected west of the Mississippi are needed just to pay the interest on the national debt. That's kind of depressing, isn't it?"

"The total national debt was only $1 trillion in 1980 when President Reagan took office. It is now $4 trillion. Maybe it was voodoo economics. Whatever it was, we are now in deep voodoo, I'll tell you that!"

Speech to the National Press Club • March 18, 1992

❑

On being included in any presidential debates:
"I could care less. Oh, I'd love to, if it's a real debate. If it's some reporter asking three candidates questions, that's not a debate. Let's just get it on; have a regular debate this year. Just like you used to in college where you've got to stand on your feet with no handlers, no cosmetologists, nobody, you know, signing you from down below, and you've got to use your head and think on your feet. I think that might be an interesting challenge for some of them."

CNN's "Larry King Live" • April 16, 1992

❑

On choosing a running mate:
"I will not just reach for an empty suit to play golf and go to funerals."

C-Span • March 23, 1992

❑

"We have government turned upside down, where the people running it act and live at your expense like royalty and many of you are working two jobs just to stay even.

"I don't know why Dan Quayle needs to take my airplane, burn up tens of thousands of dollars worth of fuel, to go play golf."

Christian Science Monitor • March 24, 1992

❑

"I challenge the incumbent President to step forward surrounded by sixteen handlers and somebody squatted down in front of him, signing and telling him what to say and when to say it. Give him all his aides. Talk about the $4 trillion debt, $3 trillion on his watch, as Vice President and President. A huge part of that $3 trillion [is] from failure to due his job in charge of deregulation around savings- and-loans and banks. Then, step forward and explain how he is going to deal with a $4 trillion debt, and why he is a part of a $400 billion increase to that debt in an election year to try to buy people's votes. Now, if the people like that, they don't want me. If they like a President who shreds, runs, ducks and hides and tries to blame minor officials, they don't want me, because I will take responsibility for my actions."

PBS's "Talking With David Frost" • April 24, 1992

❑

"At least [Gov. Bill] Clinton is out there with a platform.

"I'm not even sure the Republicans have a platform. If there's anything out there except dirty tricks and character assassination, I never heard of it."

The Dallas Morning News • *April 28, 1992*

"I think the American people will be able to figure out who can get things done and who has a record of not getting anything done and who has a record of making promises and then not delivering."

U.S. News & World Report • *May 11, 1992*

❑

And finally, eight more words from Ross Perot, recorded in the March, 30, 1992 issue of Time, that are as certain as death and Texas:

"We will not fail for lack of funds."

❑ ❑ ❑

❑ ❑

The publishing industry is not famous for its swiftness in getting a manuscript from the author's word processor into print. That this book began rolling off press 20 days after it was conceived is a tribute to many people.

The logistics of collecting the voluble Ross Perot's many recorded words from articles, books, speeches and TV transcripts were daunting.

For their ingenuity, persistence and endurance in getting it done, I thank Toby Chiu and Leslie Jay in New York, as well as Angela Thornton of Time Inc. Editorial Reference Services; Erika Sanchez in Dallas, as well as Pat Ward and Tim Wyatt; and Ken Hagen and Beverly Lyall in Annapolis, though their search of Naval Academy archives for Midshipman Perot's 1952 campaign speeches was in vain.

Anne Stovell took on the task of assembling and editing the photographs for the book, and teamed with designer Lester Goodman to display them to such handsome advantage in this small format.

The Kendig Group—Frank Kendig and Debby Gobert—proved desktop publishing to be small but beautiful. Without their talent and grace under pressure, without modems and laser printers, without the ability to go from disk directly to film (output under extreme time constraints by Thad Carr of Quad Right), I'd still be correcting galleys.

At Warner Books, I thank my editor, Mel Parker, for his faith; Amy Genkins, Esq., a writer's dream of a lawyer; and Milton Batalion and Stacey Milbauer, whose adroitness at compressing production schedules afforded me two vital extra days.

At Time Inc. Magazines, I thank Dick Stolley for his key support and for arranging my access to Edit Ref, that peerless amalgam of yellowing clips and on-line database retrievers, not to mention obscure reference works; Jennie Chien, who slashed through much red tape; and Alan Farnham for extending a Time Incer's ultimate courtesy by relinquishing precious Bio folders while himself on deadline for Fortune.

I also thank for his courtesies Jim Squires of the Dallas headquarters coordinating the multi-state Perot petition drives. At least, that was the drill in mid-May of 1992.

Tory Pryor, my literary agent, was wonderfully fierce to everyone except me.

Lastly but not least, thanks, Ali and Delia, for leading your own lives while dad worked nights.

New York City • May 16, 1992

❑ ❑